FARMING AND HOMESTEADING

WITH THE SAINTS

ANDIE ANDREWS EISENBERG

LOYOLA PRESS.
A JESUIT MINISTRY
Chicago

LOYOLAPRESS.
A JESUIT MINISTRY

www.loyolapress.com

Scripture texts in this work are taken from the *New American Bible*, revised edition © 2010, 1991, 1986, 1970 Confraternity of Christian Doctrine, Washington, D.C. All Rights Reserved.

Traditional Catholic blessings included in this work, unless otherwise noted, are taken from the *Rituale Romanum* (Roman Ritual) translated from Latin to English by Philip T. Weller, S.T.D., The Bruce Publishing Company, 1946.

Excerpts from the English translation of *The Roman Missal* © 2010, International Commission on English in the Liturgy Corporation. All rights reserved.

Cover art credit: Phecs/iStock/Getty Images, Tribalium/iStock/Getty Images, Hennadii/iStock/Getty Images, gmast3r/iStock/Getty Images.
Back cover author photo, Jillian O'Connor.

ISBN: 978-0-8294-5537-3
Library of Congress Control Number: 2023932336

Printed in the United States of America.
23 24 25 26 27 28 29 30 31 32 Versa 10 9 8 7 6 5 4 3 2 1

With gratitude . . .

To St. Isidore the Farmer,
whose example of patience, humility, and faith inspired me to keep
my hand to the plow of research and writing in the hope of bearing
fruit that will last.

To farmers everywhere,
faithful stewards of God's creation and coworkers with Christ,
who feed the world and help to renew the face of the earth.

To Our Lady of Guadalupe,
who reminds me in every season that roses in winter are possible.

Contents

Preface

I've often wondered how many Christian publishers have had manuscripts slipped under their noses with the postscript, "God told me to write this." As a writer, I know it's risky business to actually say so. However, in the legendary words of a youthful George Washington, who himself was first and foremost a farmer before becoming a president, *I cannot tell a lie*.

Three years ago, my husband and I moved westward from our tidy suburban home in New Jersey to a small farm "in the country," where I could retire my Quarter Horse, plant a garden, keep a small flock of chickens, and perhaps raise a dairy goat or two. The property was dwarfed by rolling acres of farmland that emphasized we were a hobby farm, not the "real deal." But it was our little plot of paradise, or at least we prayed it would become so once we reclaimed the land and the barn from decades of neglect.

That first year we were covered in poison ivy and regret as, armed with machetes, shovels, and rakes, we hacked away at brambles and wild vines. We tilled and reseeded the soil, hoping the pasture grasses would grow and provide for the needs of our animals. We ran water lines and planted vegetable gardens that were promptly devoured by insects we'd never seen before. Our goats dug in their cloven hooves and refused to eat the weeds. We lost our first six hens to a fox, and I wept as I plucked multicolored feathers from the wind. The barn flooded five times that first year, and with pickaxes in hand, we dug deep trenches and made peace with the rain. There was so much rain those first two years that the local farmers had a hard time producing hay fit for horses. The price increased to ten dollars per bale, and while I felt bad for my wallet, I felt worse for the farmers. My appreciation for my agricultural neighbors grew by the day with every victory and defeat we experienced on our little farm, knowing whatever we felt, they felt to a greater degree. I became increasingly humbled by and thankful for their tenacity in bringing forth gifts from the earth and for their faithful stewardship of creation, and remain deeply so.

One Friday afternoon as I sat before the Blessed Sacrament in adoration, I lamented the lack of inspiration I felt for my newest writing project. Creatively blocked and bereft at the thought of never writing again, I sulked in the shadows, tapped my foot impatiently, and said, "Okay, Lord, maybe I'm supposed to write something else. What do you want me to write?"

Farming and Homesteading with the Saints.

I let the words sink in as I scanned the kaleidoscope of stained-glass windows surrounding me, each one portraying the image of a saint in bold, triumphant colors.

"I'm a romance writer," I demurred.

Then came forth a subtitle of sorts which called for the inclusion of pertinent prayers, blessings, and scripture verses. I nodded and mulled the prospect of creating something similar to a farmer's almanac that could help those like myself seeking extra protection for their land and animals. I knew immediately that I would write the book. I felt the last three years had uniquely prepared me to do so with love and respect for modern farmers as well as for their timeless patron saints. I was, however, completely unprepared for the thousands of hours I would spend searching though ancient texts that were archived online, running documents through translation Web sites, and mining the Internet and other resources for the tiniest reference that would connect a saint to a cause. Obscurity became my archnemesis. And since quitting is my superpower, I marched back into adoration a few months later.

"It's too hard. I want to quit."

True to form, the Word of God is living and effective and it cut me to the marrow: *What if the Gospel writers had quit? What if all the monks sitting alone in their cells for years and years transcribing the Bible by hand had quit? Where would you be now?* Then he finished me off with this: *The saints are counting on you.*

And so, I humbly offer you *Farming and Homesteading with the Saints.* Though I'm not a historian by profession, I've become a lover of hagiography—in this case, the stories of saints associated with farming and homesteading that have been recorded throughout time, some as legends, some as historical fact, and some that lie in between. All of them exist for the edification of the faithful, for the exultation of the Catholic Church, and, most of all, for the glory of God.

Farming and Homesteading with the Saints is organized in five parts. Part 1 covers the creatures, critters, birds, animals, and livestock that live on or near the farm. Part 2 features saints whose specialty is the humans who care for the animals and work the land. Part 3 profiles the patron saints of places. Part 4 covers those patron saints who are known to intervene in matters concerning weather. Part 5 contains blessings and prayers for farmers and homesteaders.

This book might've been structured to resemble an encyclopedia or your typical almanac, but my own experiences of farming and homesteading urged a different approach, one that's more like farming itself: soulful and salutary, sometimes pleasantly meandering, other times intensely focused, full of surprises, and offering the occasional fence post to lean against to rest, ponder, marvel, or pray. Hence, I recommend reading this book, divided as it is into farm-friendly sections, as the Spirit moves you or as real-life circumstances lead you. What lies ahead are the indelible footprints and furrows of saints who have labored before us, in fields, barns, gardens, pastures, and paddocks, as well as in the Lord's vineyard. There's no need to plow through the pages. Enjoy the company. Take a pilgrim's journey. Pray the blessings. And take a moment (or many!) to contemplate the land and animals you love in the context of these holy men and women who understand our needs and want to intercede for us. As you wander through their stories, may you discover a patron saint—or a few—to call your own.

The intercession and example of the saints offer protection from the perils and evils of the world as we strive for heaven. Whether you're a farmer, a homesteader, a gardener, or an animal lover, I pray this book will bless your home, your farm, your fields, your barns, your animals, your heart, and your family, and bring forth fruit that will last.

In Christ's love,
Andie Andrews Eisenberg
August 15, 2022
Feast of the Assumption

Prayer to St. Isidore the Farmer

Patron of Farmers and Gardeners
Feast Day: May 15

Dear Isidore, you know how common it is to cultivate
the land,
for you were employed as a farm laborer
for the greater part of your life.

In your toils, you were blessed to receive God's help
through Angels in the fields.
O Great Saint, help all farmers and gardeners
spiritually to see the wonders God has strewn on this earth.

Encourage them in their labors
and help them to feed numerous people.
Amen.

Traditional Catholic Prayer

Part I

Patron Saints of Creatures, Critters, Flying Things, Farm Animals, and Their Ailments

When coyotes, foxes, wolves, or other predators threaten your livestock, or if you'd simply like to ensure a peaceable, healthy, happy farm, these saints have a special connection to wild and domestic animals, insects, birds, and vermin, and offer protection against related harm and diseases.

Rumination

As a hobby farmer and homesteader, it's been a challenge to navigate the mind-set between keeping livestock as pets and keeping livestock for provisions or production. In the latter case, it doesn't mean that I look at those animals with one iota less love and respect or provide them with anything less than the best, most humane life I can. As chickens fly in and out of the coop, foals are born, horses age and die, and sheep with death wishes (yes, they know a hundred ways to harm themselves) join and depart our farm family, I've had no choice but to accept the hard truth held by farmers through the ages: where there is livestock, there is dead stock.

I used to shy away from the topic. But as I settle into the land and the land settles into me, the bridge between life and death, this world and the next, the temporal and the eternal, takes on a beautiful patina akin to the burnished copper weathervane that crowns a weathered fencepost and spins like the hands of time.

There's a radiance that falls on our farm just before sunset. I call it the golden hour, and it's my favorite time of day. The chores are done. The animals are grazing in the fields. Free-ranging hens find their way back to the coop and jockey for position on the roosting bar. Everyone is present and accounted for—even those animals who have passed away, for in this golden hour, they are as near to me as lamb's breath on my cheek.

Among the hardest losses were my sweet, chocolate-colored Rocky Mountain mare and my chestnut Quarter Horse gelding—my beloved riding horse who colicked at age twenty-seven and was gone in mere hours. Both are buried behind the barn, and I often imagine them galloping with heaven's horses, chief among them the white one that will come bearing a King. My big, bad Brahma rooster is buried along the southern fence near the ladies he protected with ferocity from a hawk. We honor him and every animal we lose with a proper and prayerful goodbye in thanksgiving for the nourishment or friend-ship they provided. The sheep will enter lambing season this upcoming spring, and we pray that all will go well for them and their newborns. We know things can and do go sideways, despite the best care and intervention.

So, what does this have to do with the saints? Let's just say that I know every patron saint of the creatures in my care, and I have asked them to inter-cede for us in times of need, loss, trouble, and grief. Like portraits of favorite relatives, their pictures hang on barn walls and stall doors. An iron cross of Christ arches over all below. Granted, I don't always get the outcome I pray for, though far more often I do, but that's hardly the point. These saints know me, and I know them. There's a deep friendship forged in the mounds and furrows of joy and sorrow, and in working this farm shoulder to shoulder in their lively and holy presence. They know my animals probably better than I do. And because they also know me, they stand in the breach when I cry out with grief or fear, frustration or unknowing—and they make my requests known to God, presenting their prayers on my behalf in golden bowls . . . or maybe, in my case, in shiny feed pans.

These patron saints aren't lucky charms. They're faithful companions on the journey that is farming, homesteading, and our daily pasture walk with God. In their company, the load is lighter, the joys are sweeter, the sadness is less-ened, and their testimony that all things—even death—work for good con-soles the soul. So, I invite you to take the saints by the hand, and let them help you do the heavy lifting as you tend to your animals and every living creature on and around your farm. Rejoice in your golden hours, and always remem-ber: from wasps to worms, from birds to bees, from horses to hares and every-thing in between, there's a saint for that!

For Protection against Wild Animal Attacks

St. Blaise
Memorial: February 3

St. Blaise was a fourth-century Armenian bishop of Sebastea, Turkey, as well as a physician. Inspired by God during the persecution of Christians by the Roman emperor Licinius, St. Blaise fled to a cave outside the city, where he lived as a hermit. Wild animals, particularly those who were sick or had been wounded, sought him out and were healed by him. He lived in peace until a group of hunters who were gathering wild beasts for the purpose of devouring Christians in the amphitheater stumbled upon the hermit's cave. They were amazed at the sight of St. Blaise, who was hemmed in by wolves, lions, and bears patiently awaiting his healing ministries, kneeling in prayer. Upon seizing St. Blaise, the hunters marched him to Agricolaus, who was the bloodthirsty governor of Cappadocia and Lesser Armenia. Along the way to prison, St. Blaise encountered a woman whose pig was being carried off by a wolf. St. Blaise commanded the wolf to release the pig, and it was freed unharmed, again to the amazement of all. He was tortured and beheaded around 316.

St. Blaise is one of a group of saints invoked for their powerful role against plagues and sudden death and whose intercession is especially powerful. Known as the Fourteen Holy Helpers, these saints include St. Acathius (also known as Acacius), St. Barbara, St. Catherine of Alexandria, St. Christopher, St. Cyriacus (also known as Cyriac), St. Denis, St. Erasmus (also known as Elmo), St. Eustace, St. George, St. Giles, St. Margaret of Antioch, St. Pantaleon, St. Vitus (also known as Guy), and, of course, St. Blaise. All but St. Giles were martyred.

See also pages 52, 59, 101, and 126.

St. Vitus

Memorial: June 15

The son of a wealthy Italian senator, St. Vitus was baptized as a boy by his tutor and his attendant without his parents' knowledge. Being pure of heart, he obtained many miracles and conversions in his hometown, which enraged not only his father but also the powerful administrator of Sicily. Their threats and punishments, including imprisonment, failed to shake St. Vitus's commitment to the Christian faith. Guided by angels and divine inspiration, he escaped from prison and, along with his tutor and his attendant, fled to Lucania. There, the threesome preached the gospel and were said to have been fed and protected from fierce storms by an eagle. They journeyed to Rome, where St. Vitus cured the possessed son of the Roman emperor Diocletian. Rather than expressing gratitude for the healing, Diocletian charged St. Vitus with practicing sorcery. He demanded that St. Vitus make a sacrifice to his pagan gods. When St. Vitus refused, Diocletian ordered him to be fed to a lion. The lion refused to harm St. Vitus. Instead, the lion crouched before him and licked his feet. St. Vitus was martyred in 303 after being boiled in oil and tortured on a rack.

See also pages 18 and 135–36.
See also page 204 for a Deprecatory Blessing against Pests.

For Protection against Wolves and Foxes

While there's no official patron saint for protection against wolf attacks, the following patron saints of wolves (and foxes) ought to be invoked.

St. Ailbe of Emly

Memorial: September 12

St. Ailbe was a preacher, a bishop, a disciple of St. Patrick, and one of Ireland's most beloved saints. Legend has it that as an infant, St. Ailbe was abandoned in the woods, but survived because he was suckled by a wolf. Years later, in his travels as a missionary preacher, an old she-wolf came to St. Ailbe for protection from a hunting party. As she rested her head affectionately upon his chest, St. Ailbe recognized her as the wolf who had fostered him. He saved her from the hunters and thereafter provided for her every need.

In his position as the first bishop of Emly, he was known for his holiness and intelligence. He is considered one of the fathers of the Irish church. Today's farmers can invoke St. Ailbe to use his legendary influence and friendship with wolves to keep them out of the sheepfold. St. Ailbe died in 541 of natural causes and is often depicted in art with a wolf or wolf pack.

St. Edmund of East Anglia
Memorial: November 20

An Anglo-Saxon king who ruled in 855–869, St. Edmund was taken hostage in a battle with Viking raiders. According to legend, when he refused to renounce his Christian faith, he was tortured by being shot through with so many arrows he resembled a hedgehog. He was beheaded while barely alive and his head was tossed into the deep brush and briars of the forest. When the Saxon warriors who survived the battle returned to the scene looking for their king, they found only his decapitated body. Their search for the head of their king was futile until they heard a beckoning cry. Following the sound, they came upon a large gray wolf, who held St. Edmund's head between its paws, guarding it from harm. When the head was reunited with the body, it miraculously reattached as though it had never been severed, giving rise to his cult as England's original patron saint and a patron saint of wolves.

St. Hervé
Memorial: June 17

St. Hervé, a native of Brittany, France (alternately, Wales) was born blind, lost his father at a young age, and was raised throughout his teens by his devout uncle, who was an abbot. St. Hervé became a monk, teacher, and beloved traveling musician who was known for working miracles and healing animals. Legend holds that one day while St. Hervé and his student-guide were plowing a field, a wolf sprang from the underbrush and killed and devoured St. Hervé's plowing ox (alternately, donkey). St. Hervé chastised the wolf and preached to it. In response, the wolf meekly took the oxen's place at the plow. So great was his connection to animals that in his later years, St. Hervé kept as a companion a wolf that served as his sight-guide. St. Hervé died in the mid-sixth century.

In Brittany, St. Hervé's influence is so prevalent, Breton mothers threaten disobedient children with a visit from St. Hervé's wolf. Occasionally, St. Hervé is depicted with a fox, as he is also credited with having rescued one of his own hens from the jaws of a fox that released the bird at St. Hervé's command.

For Protection against Bears

*An unofficial patron saint of bears, St. Corbinian can be
invoked for protection against attacks by bears on poultry,
livestock, and humans.*

St. Corbinian
Memorial: September 8

Born around 670 near Chartres, France, little is known of St. Corbinian's youth. As a young man, he resided in a hermit's cell for fourteen years, but his reputation for holiness and wonderworking gradually attracted many followers. He founded a hermitage near Chartres and became known as a gifted teacher and spiritual director. He had a great devotion to St. Peter the apostle, which prompted him to set out on a pilgrimage to Rome. Along the way, according to legend, St. Corbinian's pack horse or mule was attacked and killed by a bear. The saint sternly reprimanded the bear, set the mule's saddle on its back, and commanded it to carry his provisions for the rest of the journey. Upon reaching Rome, the bear was released and returned to its native home. While in Rome, St. Corbinian was ordained a missionary bishop and sent to Bavaria, Germany, to evangelize in the vicinity of Freising. St. Corbinian died of natural causes in 730. He is often depicted in art with a saddled bear and a mule.

For Protection against Mosquitoes and Biting Flies

Are winged pests, hungry caterpillars, burrowing ticks, or other damaging insects getting the best of you, your livestock, or your crops? Here are some saints whose prayers handily dispatch biting, stinging, crawling, and flying things.

St. Narcissus of Girona
Memorial: October 29

A fourth-century priest, preacher, and bishop of Girona, Spain, St. Narcissus and his deacon, St. Felix, also of Girona, fled to Germany and Switzerland to escape the persecution of Christians during the reign of the Roman emperor Diocletian. While in exile, St. Narcissus preached to the barbarians in the Swiss canton of Grisons. He also evangelized in the region of Augsburg, in Germania. Upon his return to Girona, he and St. Felix were arrested. Sources report the year of St. Narcissus's martyrdom variously as either 304 or 307.

Girona, which is a border town in northern Spain near the Pyrenees mountains, has a long history of squabbles with neighboring France. In 1286, the French army marched into town intent on sacking Girona and laying siege to its treasures. Upon entering the church of St. Felix, soldiers made a terrible tactical blunder by ransacking the tomb of St. Narcissus. At that moment, a massive swarm of stinging, biting flies burst forth from the tomb, flew all throughout the city, and mercilessly attacked every French soldier. Panic and mayhem ensued. The enemy retreated from the city and peace was restored to Girona.

The city of Girona honors St. Narcissus's feast day with a ten-day festival where souvenirs resembling flies abound. An ornamental concrete fly on a city wall is accompanied by a plaque written in Catalan that invites visitors to *Acaricia les mosques de Sant Narcís i demana el teu miracle*, that is, "Pat the flies of St. Narcissus and ask for a miracle."

For Protection against Wasps

St. Friard
Memorial: August 1

Born in 511, St. Friard is also the patron saint of people suffering from *sphek-sophobia*, which is the fear of wasps. St. Friard was a hermit who lived on the island of Vindomitte, France. As the story goes, his piety was both scorned and envied, and one day the locals set out to torment him. As they converged upon him, a swarm of wasps came to St. Friard's defense, pestering and stinging his assailants. St. Friard, being a good and holy man, prayed for his tormentors, and the wasps retreated at the sound of his prayer. Another version portrays St. Friard as a farm laborer who, when harvesting a crop of corn with his fellow farmhands, was pestered in the cornfield by a swarm of wasps. His coworkers, who often made a mockery of St. Friard's devotions, said to him, "Friard, you are always making the sign of the cross on your eyes, ears, and mouth; why don't you drive off these devils with the sign of the cross?" Thinking it a marvelous opportunity to win souls for the Lord, St. Friard knelt in the cornfield and silently prayed to God that the wasps would disappear. Rising to his feet, he said, "Work on now; these insects will trouble you no more." At that, the wasps flew away. St. Friard followed them, saying, *Ajutorium nostrum in nomine Domini* ("Our help is in the name of God"). The swarm of wasps was said to have entered a hole in the ground, never to be seen in the cornfields again. This display of faith in the power of God made a big impression on his coworkers, who thereafter regarded his devotions with great respect. St. Friard died in 577 of natural causes.

For Protection against Caterpillars

St. Magnus of Füssen
Memorial: September 6

Legend has it that St. Magnus, a sixth-century Benedictine missionary saint who lived in southern Germany, single-handedly dispatched a family of dragons so that a monastery could be built on the plot of land they occupied. A prudent and wise man, he kept one baby dragon alive to hunt rodents and other crop-damaging pests, including caterpillars and grubs, that troubled the local farmers and had a negative impact on their food supply. St. Magnus died of natural causes in about 750.

Later, in the seventeenth and eighteenth centuries, the crosier of St. Magnus, which was preserved in the cloister of St. Mang at Füssen in Bavaria, was borne in solemn procession to Lucerne, Zug, Schwyz, and other portions of Switzerland for the expulsion and extermination of rats, mice, cockchafers, and other field insects, especially hungry caterpillars.

See also page 172.

For Protection against Spiders

St. Felix of Nola
Memorial: January 14
Want to keep spiders from spinning their highly combustible webs in the dark corners and rafters of your outbuildings, barns, or even your house? Want to be spared from a painful bite? St. Felix is a powerful saint who covers the more than thirty thousand known species of spiders.

St. Felix was a third-century Christian who was being pursued by Roman soldiers for the bold practice of his faith. It is told that he ducked into a vacant building to hide from his persecutors. Once inside, spiders quickly spun elaborate webs over the doorway, giving the Roman soldiers the impression that the building was long uninhabited. As the bishop of Nola, Italy, St. Felix was arrested along with thirty other Christians and martyred around 287 under the persecution of the Roman prefect Marcianus.

For the General Protection against and Fear of Insects

St. Gratus of Aosta
Memorial: September 7

Among his many miracles, St. Gratus, a fifth-century Italian bishop of noble birth, is said to have thwarted a plague of grasshoppers by his prayers. Later, in the 1400s, his name was invoked when the Tarentaise region of France was infested with a devastating plague of insects. A threefold blessing ceremony of the earth, water, and candles (remnants of a pagan ritual that later became Christianized and attached to St. Gratus) coincides with the beginning of spring. Today, St. Gratus is invoked to ward off pestilence from fields, farmers, and livestock, and to petition for God's favor on the growing crops. St. Gratus died of natural causes around 470 in Aosta, Italy.

See also pages 151 and 171.

St. Tryphon of Lampsacus
Memorial: February 1

Born in the third century to Christian parents, St. Tryphon's father died when Tryphon was a young child. He helped his mother by working as a gooseherd in the fields of Phrygia, in modern-day Turkey. It is said that when Tryphon was a boy, the sound of his voice raised in prayer caused a swarm of locusts descending on the village's grain fields to take flight, thus sparing the farmers' crops from harm. As a pious youth, he was known for his gift of healing animals and humans as well as for his gift of evangelization. He converted many pagan imperial officials to the Christian faith, which enraged the Roman emperor Decius, who had him arrested, tortured, and killed in 250.

See also pages 63 and 108–09.

For Protection against Rodents

*Whether they're chewing electrical cords in your barn or the
wiring of your farm equipment, nesting in your truck, gnawing
on the baling twine that binds your hay, burrowing holes,
getting into the feed, ravaging your pantry, destroying crops, or
spreading disease, rodents are arguably the most destructive and
prolific pests that plague a farm. Call on these saints for a
divine method of pest control.*

St. Gertrude of Nivelles
Memorial: March 17

The daughter of nobility, St. Gertrude of Nivelles (not to be confused with St. Gertrude the Great) was born around 626 in what is now Belgium. She became the abbess of a Benedictine monastery in Nivelles, Belgium, where she exercised a special devotion to praying for the souls in purgatory. Her other specialty is the eradication of field mice. She is said to have driven field mice out of the land by her prayers, thereby protecting people from disease and sparing the farmers' crops. Water from her abbey's well and morsels of the bread she baked were scattered about to repel both mice and rats. Her name is invoked against vermin, rats, and mice, as well as against *murophobia*, which is the fear of mice or rats.

St. Gertrude of Nivelles is often portrayed as an abbess with mice running up her pastoral staff or cloak. Some say this symbolizes her devotion to the souls in purgatory since, according to Teutonic tradition, these souls were often depicted as mice. As recently as the 1800s, offerings of mice made of gold and silver were placed at her shrine in Cologne. Of course, her depiction with mice as well as with a cat is also symbolic of her powerful intercession in thwarting epidemics and protecting farmers' crops from mice and other vermin. St. Gertrude of Nivelles died at the same age as Christ, just thirty-three years old, in 659.

See also pages 37 and 107.

St. Martin de Porres
Memorial: November 3

Invoked primarily against rats, St. Martin was born in Lima, Peru, in 1579 to a Spanish nobleman and a freed black slave, Anna Velasquez. Considered illegitimate by birth and raised in deep poverty, it is not surprising that he became a servant. Later, he became a Dominican brother in the Holy Rosary priory in Lima. Legend has it that when the priory became infested with hundreds of mice and rats, St. Martin held a meeting with the unruly rodents in the outdoor garden. He told them the prior had instructed him to set out poison, which he was obligated to do, but that if they remained outdoors, he would feed them every day in the barn. Both parties abided by the agreement, and the priory was no longer troubled by rats.

St. Martin died in Peru in 1639 of fever. In 1962 he became the first black person from the Americas to be canonized. He is often depicted holding a broom, with a dog, cat, and mouse at his feet.

St. Servatus of Tongres
Memorial: May 13

St. Servatus was an Armenian nobleman by birth who was said to be a distant relative to Christ. He was esteemed for his learning and holiness. As bishop of Tongres/Tongeren in Belgium, then part of Gaul, St. Servatus was a staunch defender of the Catholic faith against the Arians in the mid-fourth century. He undertook a penitential pilgrimage to Rome to stave off the destruction of Gaul, an event of which he'd been divinely foretold. Upon his return, he fell into the hands of barbarians who tried to put him to death as he slept. However, he was shielded by a fierce eagle who overshadowed him with its wings, thereby protecting him from his assailants as well as from the hot sun. For this reason, he is generally associated with an eagle, whose steady diet of mice and rats likely led to the saint's loose association with protection against rodents. St. Servatus died of a fever in Tongres, Belgium, in 384.

St. Ulric of Augsburg
Memorial: July 4

A descendent from a long line of German nobles, St. Ulric was educated from the time he was seven years old in the abbey of St. Gall. As bishop of Augsburg, in 923, he was known for setting high standards of moral conduct and social responsibility, as evidenced by his dedication to building churches, tending to the sick in hospitals, and pastoring his flock. He was the first saint to be formally canonized by a pope.

Following his death in 973 of natural causes, some of St. Ulric's relics were deposited in a monastery in Ardennes in southeast Belgium, where the friars boasted that no rats took up residence in their home or neighborhood owing to the presence of the relics. Earth from St. Ulric's grave in Augsburg is said to have the power to repel rodents, and many pilgrims have collected dirt from his place of rest for that purpose. Unsurprisingly, then, he is also invoked against rats and moles. Tradition has it that the touch of this bishop's pastoral cross was used to heal people bitten by rabid dogs.

For Protection against Snakes and Snakebites

While nonvenomous snakes are beneficial to have around because they consume rodents, chipmunks, gophers, and even insects, venomous snakes make unwelcome guests. They can lurk in and around chicken coops, hay bales, rock walls, ponds, woodpiles, old cisterns, and other hiding places. Invoking the patron saints who have banished poisonous snakes or escaped harm from them can help keep the deadly ones at bay.

St. Hilary of Poitiers
Memorial: January 13

Born to pagan parents around 300, St. Hilary was a husband and father. As a nobleman, he was self-directed in the pursuit of religious and academic knowledge. Upon discovering and reading the New Testament, he eagerly converted to Christianity. Because of his zeal for and knowledge of the Christian faith, he was later ordained as the bishop of Poitiers, France, where he served from 353 until his death in 368. He was declared a doctor of the church in 1851.

Having traveled far and wide to the point of exile for the purpose of combatting Arianism, St. Hilary is said to have merely set foot on the snake-infested island of Gallinara, near Andora, Italy, and the resident snakes fled in terror. He marked a line of separation by planting his crosier in the earth so that the snakes were banished to the area beyond and the rest of the island would be safe for human habitation.

Our Lady of Madhu
Memorial: July 2

The miraculous statue of Our Lady of Madhu, a representation of the Virgin Mary that resides on the island of Sri Lanka, dates to the seventeenth century. Catholics who were fleeing the persecution of the colonial Dutch in the city of Mantai enshrined the statue in Madhu, a jungle village where many species of snakes thrive. Located 185 miles from the capital of Colombo, pilgrims to Our Lady of Madhu venerate her as the Queen of Snakes and invoke her protection against deadly snakebites. An opening cut into the floor of the church near the altar gives pilgrims access to soil that is said to be an antidote for snakebites. The soil is also sometimes mixed into the concrete used in pouring the foundations of the villagers' homes for protection against snake infestations.

St. Patrick
Memorial: March 17

Born in Scotland in the late fourth century, St. Patrick escaped bondage and began his formal religious education and formation in monasteries throughout Europe. He became a priest, then a bishop, and was sent by Pope Celestine to evangelize first England and then Ireland. He was known as a wonderworker who converted thousands of pagans in the course of his adventurous life. He died of natural causes in the mid-fifth century.

St. Patrick is said to have chased Ireland's entire population of snakes into the sea after they attacked him on a hilltop during his forty-day spiritual retreat. Some say the ouster of snakes was merely a metaphor for the zeal with which St. Patrick set about ridding the island of paganism, which was often symbolized by a snake. The Druid culture, however, was well known for its serpent worship. Perhaps the truth of the matter lies somewhere in the middle.

See also pages 150–51.

St. Paul the Apostle
Memorial: June 29

Saul of Tarsus was a first-century Pharisee, a tentmaker by trade, and a contemporary of the apostles who was known for his early persecution of Christians. He took a prominent role in the stoning of St. Stephen, the first martyr for the faith. Around 33, having been struck by a blinding light on the road to Damascus in pursuit of Christian "heretics," Saul of Tarsus, whom we know today as St. Paul, experienced a profound conversion.

While shipwrecked on the island of Malta, St. Paul was gathering a bundle of brushwood and putting it on the fire when, driven out by the heat, a viper latched onto his hand. When the native islanders saw the snake hanging from his flesh, they exclaimed, "This man must certainly be a murderer; though he escaped the sea, Justice has not let him remain alive." But St. Paul simply "shook the snake off into the fire and suffered no harm" (Acts 28:3–5). Hence St. Paul is invoked against poisonous snakes. St. Paul was martyred in 67 in Rome, Italy.

See also pages 100–01 and 186.

St. Phocas the Gardener
Memorial: July 3 (alternately, also July 23 and September 22)

A humble farmer, innkeeper, and gardener, St. Phocas was known for using his surplus crops to feed the local poor, which he did in the name of Christ. The local authorities, having heard there was a Christian living nearby, sent two Roman soldiers to execute him. The soldiers threw him into a pit with venomous snakes, but the snakes refused to bite him.

Invoked against snakebites, St. Phocas is traditionally depicted holding the palm of martyrs with many serpents entwined around his arms. St. Phocas was beheaded in 303 in Sinope, Pontus, in modern-day Turkey.

See also pages 82 and 107.

St. Vitus
Memorial: June 15

St. Vitus is well known for his patronage of those who suffer from epilepsy and other nervous disorders and diseases, particularly those that manifest in abnormal movements of the body, known as "St. Vitus' Dance." By association, he has become known as a patron saint against snakebites, presumably those with venoms that would affect the nervous system.

See also pages 6 and 135–36.
See also page 204 for a Deprecatory Blessing against Pests.

For Protection against Rabies and Its Carriers

St. Bellinus of Padua
Memorial: November 26

St. Bellinus was a twelfth-century bishop of Padua, Italy, who was reported variously to have been martyred by a pack of vicious dogs or assassinated on his way to Rome. In the basilica that houses his remains, an altar pall painted by Italian painter Mattia Bortoloni depicts the bishop with his staff and his keys as he protects a boy from a rabid dog. Custom has it that someone sickened by the bite of a rabid dog could be cured by entering through one door of this church and exiting through another. It is also said that an order of nuns in Padua possesses the "key of St. Bellino," which when heated and pressed to the head of a mad dog was curative to the animal and thereby also a blessing to the townspeople. Some say that the same procedure was also used to cure humans.

St. Bieuzy of Brittany
Memorial: November 24

A monk and spiritual protégé of the Irish monk St. Gildas the Wise, St. Bieuzy followed his mentor in his work preaching to pagans throughout Brittany, France. He was known for his gifts of healing people and animals, and, in particular, for his ability to miraculously cure those stricken with rabies, which was a widespread disease in the sixth and seventh centuries. Sometime in the seventh century, things came to a bad ending for St. Bieuzy. When he refused to interrupt a sermon to cure a rabid dog belonging to a local chief, the chief struck him down with an axe. Water that miraculously springs from the spot in Pluvigner, France, where St. Beiuzy was martyred is said to cure sickness resulting from dog bites.

St. Denis of Paris
Memorial: October 9

A zealous missionary and the first bishop of Paris, France, St. Denis is one of the church's Fourteen Holy Helpers. In retaliation for his impassioned preaching and widespread conversion of pagans, he was imprisoned by the Roman governor and beheaded in 258. Roughly 250 years later, King Clovis, a barbarian-turned-Christian, reportedly demanded that the monks of the Abbey of St. Denis open the martyr's tomb so that he could view the relics. Perhaps his barbaric tendencies got the better of him when he reached into the stone sarcophagus, seized a piece of bone, and walked out of the church with it. Soon after desecrating the relics, he went insane, his madness giving rise to St. Denis's loose association with the healing of rabies.

St. Hubert of Liège
Memorial: November 3

After his conversion to Christianity during a hunting expedition, St. Hubert evangelized the Ardennes region of France throughout the late seventh and early eighth centuries. Long venerated as a patron saint of hunters and trappers, he has been invoked against rabies and bad behavior in dogs, particularly hunting dogs, from as early as the ninth century.

When, in 826, St. Hubert's thigh bone was transferred to a Belgium abbey located near Liège, Belgium, the abbey became famous as a center for rabies prevention. It was customary at this time to brand the skin of dogs with a white-hot "Key of St. Hubert" so that they would not contract the disease. The key was also heated and pressed to the dog's bite wound as a means of sterilization, cauterization, and healing following a bite by a rabid animal. In humans, however, such branding was eventually considered too extreme and too unreliable, so humans were protected from rabies infection following a bite by planting threads from St. Hubert's reportedly miraculous stole into an incision made at the site of the bite, and accompanied by much prayer and fasting.

See also pages 39–40.

St. Otto of Bamberg
Memorial: July 2

A humble priest of noble birth who became, in the twelfth century, the Bishop of Bamberg, Germany, St. Otto founded twenty new monasteries and reformed existing communities. He himself embraced a monastic lifestyle, shunning the luxuries of his position, choosing instead to use financial resources for the care of the poor. His concern for the poor as well as people in religious orders earned him the moniker "Father of Monks." He is said to have converted twenty thousand pagans with the evangelizing work he did in Poland. St. Otto died in 1139. His ornate, raised tomb was fashioned with a low, arched opening below it, through which pilgrims crawl to come into closer contact with the saint, giving rise to his protection against backaches (a significant benefit to hardworking farmers!).

A special "Otto wine" was given to pilgrims at the Otto altar to protect them against fever and rabies, stemming from the tale of a soldier whose wild behavior inspired concerned friends to bring him to a location where St. Otto was known to pray and celebrate Mass. The friends hoisted the soldier onto a wooden table. After lying there for some time, the soldier sprang up, healed of his affliction, and expressed immense gratitude toward God and the bishop. St. Otto is frequently depicted in art as a bishop with a dog.

St. Peter Chrysologus
Memorial: July 30

St. Peter Chrysologus (meaning "golden word") was born in Imola, Italy. He was an adult convert to Christianity, as well as a deacon, priest, and then, in 433, bishop of Ravenna, Italy. St. Peter was known for his eloquent preaching; 176 of the sermons he wrote survive today. Around 450, when he returned to Imola, he was welcomed home with gifts of a gold chalice and a silver patten. He was buried in the church of St. Cassian.

A local parish priest reported in 1642 that many people came to Imola to venerate the remains of the saint, and some who drank water from his paten were healed of various fevers as well as from the bites of rabid dogs. St. Peter was proclaimed a doctor of the church in 1729.

St. Sithney
Memorial: August 4

A sixth-century emigrant from Britain, St. Sithney founded a monastery in Brittany, France, that was distinguished by a miraculous well. Legend has it that when God asked St. Sithney to be the patron of girls seeking husbands, he replied in exasperation that he would never get any rest and would rather take care of mad dogs than women! God granted his request; since then, mad dogs have been given water from St. Sithney's well as a cure. St. Sithney died in 529 of natural causes.

For Protection against Worms and Parasites

St. Benignus of Armagh
Memorial: November 9

The son of an Irish chieftain, St. Benignus and his family were converted to Christianity by St. Patrick. Not surprisingly, St. Benignus saw St. Patrick as a hero of the faith, and longed to become his disciple. Despite his youth, St. Patrick agreed to allow young St. Benignus to accompany him on his missionary travels. Following in his mentor's footsteps, St. Benignus became a priest who succeeded St. Patrick as the archbishop of Ireland.

In his old age, St. Benignus is said to have traveled to Glastonbury at the urging of an angel so that he could be reunited with St. Patrick. There, St. Patrick instructed him to travel onward until he arrived at a place where his staff put forth buds and bloomed. This would indicate where his final resting place was meant to be. St. Benignus's staff bloomed on the lonely Isle of Feringmere, located in the marshlands. There, he lived out the remainder of his life in a cell as a hermit, dying in 467 of natural causes. Six centuries later, in 1091, his body was said to have been translated to a church at Glastonbury. A throng of the faithful had gathered to receive it, and "several persons who were troubled with intestinal worms threw them up in the sight of the congregation." His patronage against worms and parasites was thus cemented.

St. Mawes
Memorial: November 18

A sixth-century missionary monk of Welsh origin, St. Mawes lived the eremitical life in Cornwall, where he founded a fishing village and became its patron. He also founded a monastery on the island of Maudez, off the coast of Brittany, where he lived as an abbot. He banished snakes and vermin from Maudez by setting fire to the grass. Perhaps this led to his association with protection against worms, as any parasites infecting the land would have perished as well. Following his peaceful death, he is said to have worked many miracles ridding people of parasitic worms and diseases.

For Protection against Equine Diseases and for Equine Health

St. Eligius of Noyon
Memorial: December 1

St. Eligius (known in England as St. Loy) was born in France around 590. His extraordinary skill as a metalsmith caught the attention of King Clotaire II, and he was appointed the master of the mint. As his fame and fortune spread, he used his wealth and influence to build churches and convents and to ransom slaves. Later in life, he was ordained to the priesthood and became a beloved bishop of Noyon.

St. Eligius's reputation as a patron of horses and the people who work with them stems largely from *The Life of Eligius*, written by Dado, who was Eligius's friend and the bishop of nearby Rouen. The story is told, with some variation as to whether the horse was given or bequeathed, that St. Eligius kept a horse who was as kind and gentle as he was. In his role as the bishop of Noyon, St. Eligius traveled on horseback throughout the region visiting the sick and the poor, to whom he was deeply devoted. His horse was widely admired for steadiness of strength and willingness in disposition.

Eligius fell sick with a mortal fever in 660, and his beloved horse was bequeathed to the abbot presiding over the basilica of St. Paul (which St. Eligius had built during his episcopacy). However, when the new bishop of Noyon was installed, he coveted the fine horse and took it for his own from the abbot. The abbot dared not complain. Instead, he commended his cause to St. Eligius. Shortly afterward, the horse began to suffer "a sickness of the feet" and its body began "withering" and "wasting." The bishop called in a mule doctor, who could offer no cure. The horse reacted to people with the wildness of a beast. Worried that the horse would die, the bishop gave the horse to a kind matron whom he thought might have better success with it. She attempted to ride the horse, was violently thrown, and indignantly brought the horse right back. At that point, the bishop was advised by a local priest to simply return the horse to the abbot. When the horse was returned, it miraculously and instantly regained its former vigor and gentle disposition, which the abbot attributed to the intercession of his dear friend St. Eligius. From this story stems St. Eligius's association with the curing of equine disease of every kind.

See also pages 44, 99, 101, and 132.
See also page 220 for a Blessing of Salt or Oats for Animals.

For the General Protection against Diseased Cattle

St. Beuno Gasulsych
Memorial: April 21

St. Beuno was the grandson of Welsh royalty; there are those who maintain that he is the grandnephew of King Arthur. At any rate, he was born in 545 and was ordained to the priesthood in Bangor, Wales. He founded a monastery in Clynnog Fawr, in North Wales, where he served as abbot. There, he was said to have miraculously raised seven people from the dead. He died of natural causes around 640.

From late medieval times, intercessory services for sick livestock were regularly held at St. Beuno's Church, owing to reports that the saint's own cattle had always done well there. Until the early nineteenth century, it was customary for farmers to bring their sick cattle to Ffynnon Feuno, a holy well dedicated to St. Beuno that was located two hundred yards from the church. When the livestock drank the water, they were said to be miraculously healed of their disorders. Also during that time, young lambs and calves that were born with a slit in their ear (a condition called St. Beuno's Mark that was thought to identify these creatures as sacred beasts) were brought by farmers to the church to be donated and sold. The proceeds were deposited into Cyff Beuno (Beuno's Chest) and used toward doing corporal works of mercy.

St. Erhard of Regensburg
Memorial: January 8

Born in Ireland in the seventh century, St. Erhard served as the bishop of Ardagh before becoming a missionary to Bavaria, Germany, and then the bishop of Regensburg. He was a miracle worker who restored the sight of St. Odilia, who had been born blind. He founded and then retired to a monastery in Regensburg. Following his death of natural causes around 686, many miracles occurred at his tomb, which at the time was guarded by a community of nuns who offered perpetual prayer. While his association with livestock is obscure, it's known that during the eighteenth to the twentieth centuries in Germany, images of him were offered to sick animals as *Schluckbildchen*, which is a kind of curative folk medicine whereby a paper pill with an image of a saint imprinted on it (in this case, of St. Erhard) was either soaked and dissolved in water or added to food, and then swallowed by the sick human or animal.

See also page 99.
See also page 199 for a Blessing of Sick Animals.

St. Gerlac of Valkenburg
Memorial: January 5

Born to a noble family around 1100 in the Netherlands, St. Gerlac was a depraved soldier in the German army and a thief in his youth. Following the death of his wife, he became a devout Christian and undertook penitential pilgrimages to Rome and Jerusalem. In Rome, he nursed the sick for seven years. Upon his return to the Netherlands, he divested his wealth and became a hermit in the base of a massive hollowed-out oak tree that grew on his estate in Valkenburg, in the province of Limberg (Netherlands). As a hermit, he sustained himself on bread mixed with ash and water from a nearby well. He died sometime in the 1170s of natural causes and is often depicted as a man surrounded by farmers and cattle.

His namesake church is in the same area and is the site of his tomb. In a space beneath the tomb is a heap of "blessed sand" (actually, limestone powder) along with plastic bags and a small trowel. Pilgrims use the blessed sand to cure their sick livestock. Sprinkling the sand in the stalls is said to keep horses and cattle healthy, and spreading it in the fields is said to keep mice and rats out of the corn.

Healing power is also attributed to water from St. Gerlac's well, as well as from the timber of the mighty oak. Soil collected from his original grave site is mixed with water and used as medicine for people and animals alike, especially for rubbing between the horns of the cattle for healing or protection.

For Protection against Mad Cow Disease

St. Saturninus of Toulouse
Memorial: November 29

Born in Greece in the third century to Roman nobility, St. Saturninus was a missionary who preached the gospel and converted many to the faith in southern Gaul. He became the first bishop of Toulouse, France, and, under the persecutions of Valerian, was seized in 257 by leaders of the pagan temple who exercised a particular devotion to the bull-gods. He was given an ultimatum to either worship their gods or pay with his life. St. Saturninus replied, "I adore only one God, and to him I am ready to offer a sacrifice of praise. Your gods are devils and are more delighted with the sacrifice of your souls than with those of your bullocks." Enraged, the mob whipped him, then tethered him to a bull that was to be sacrificed. They prodded and teased the animal before setting it loose. The maddened bull dragged St. Saturninus through the streets. His skull was broken, and he died. The bull continued to gallop until the ropes to which the corpse was tied snapped.

Christians of the Toulouse community constructed the Church of the Taur ("Church of the Bull") at the very spot where the body of St. Saturnius was no longer subjected to the maniacal bull run. That church, since then renamed Notre-Dame du Taur, stands even today in Toulouse.

For the General Protection of Animals and Lost Animals

Throughout the ages, farm animals from horses to sheep, goats, cattle, swine, and everything in between have received the aid of the saints. The following saints are closely connected to farm life and to the needs of our domestic animal friends, workers, and companions.

St. Anthony of Padua
Memorial: June 13

Born in 1195 in Lisbon, Portugal, St. Anthony relinquished his family's wealth, choosing to become first an Augustinian priest, then a Franciscan. He was gifted in preaching and teaching, and was recognized by his superior, St. Francis of Assisi, as being especially blessed with these gifts. He was sent to evangelize throughout northern Italy and France. He died in 1231 of natural causes, and it is said that the sick who visited his fresh grave in Padua were miraculously healed. He was proclaimed a doctor of the church in 1946.

Perhaps it was his close association with St. Francis that gave rise to his general patronage of domestic animals, or perhaps it was the result of miracles worked at his tomb. More likely, it comes from his profound connectedness with all of God's creation, as demonstrated by his famous sermon delivered to a massive school of fish. When the local heretics of Rimini, Italy, refused to listen to his homilies, St. Anthony did not dwell on their rejection. Instead, he went to the banks of the nearby Marecchia River, where he beckoned the fish. They came to him by the thousands, breaching the water so that they could hear the messages of God's grace and goodness he shared with them.

St. Anthony is often invoked as the patron saint of lost objects; this also includes lost animals. The association stems from a story about the sudden disappearance of St. Anthony's psalter, in which were stashed a treasury of his notes and teachings. He grieved the loss of this cherished possession and prayed that it would be found. As it turned out, the psalter had been stolen by a disgruntled novice, who meekly returned it after experiencing a vision of an angry St. Anthony. The stolen psalter is reportedly being kept safe in a Franciscan friary in Bologna, in northern Italy.

See also pages 53, 58, and 144.
See also page 197 for the Prayer of St. Anthony.
See also page 203 for the Prayer to St. Anthony for Lost Animals.

For the General Protection of Domestic Animals

St. Anthony the Abbot
Memorial: January 17

Born in Egypt in 251 to a wealthy family, St. Anthony the Abbot (and, alternately, St. Anthony of Egypt) was orphaned at the age of twenty, which is when he decided to give all his possessions to the poor. Having founded the first Christian monastery, in Palestine, he is considered the Father of Monks. Centuries later, St. Benedict modeled his own monastery upon St. Anthony's Palestinian monastery.

St. Anthony lived as a hermit in the desert in a rock-hewn tomb, and later in the ruins of a mountaintop fort where he kept long periods of fasting and penance. He died of natural causes in 356.

In Christian art, he is frequently represented with a pig at his side. It is believed that he kept close company with animals, giving rise to his distinction as the patron saint of domestic animals and farm stock. Some people believe that on the night of St. Anthony's feast, the animals are able to speak—but it's best that the farmers don't hear the things they have to say. Traditionally, on his feast day or the Sunday nearest, animals throughout the world, including cattle, pigs, and horses, are blessed and placed under his protection. Farmers and farmhands who seek his intercession are quite devoted to St. Anthony, and his image is frequently placed above stable doors.

A story is told of a small town near Assisi, Italy, *Santa Maria degli Angeli*, which was a transit stop for the postal service and commerce between Florence and Rome. There, horses were fed and watered or swapped out for fresh horses. Around 1860, a serious epidemic affecting horses broke out and threatened commerce to the point of collapse. Because his feast day was near, the faithful called on St. Anthony the Abbot for his intercession. Their prayers were successful in eradicating the epidemic.

See also pages 57–58, 86, and 96.
See also page 200 for a Blessing of Horses and Other Animals.

St. Francis of Assisi
Memorial: October 4

Arguably the most well-known patron saint of animals, St. Francis began his life as Giovanni di Pietro di Bernadone in Assisi, Umbria (now part of Italy) in 1181. The son of a wealthy cloth merchant, a misspent youth culminated in 1202 when he joined the local militia. He was injured in battle, and was taken prisoner of war. During his year-long imprisonment, he experienced visions from God which inspired a deep conversion. Upon his release, he renounced his wealth and status to become, in his words, a "beggar for Christ." His zeal and mission to serve the sick, the poor, and the vulnerable inspired other men to join him in forming the Franciscan Order. St. Francis suffered the stigmata in 1224, and died of natural causes two years later.

Tales of Francis's love for all God's creatures abound. He considered all animals to be his brethren. He preached sermons to the birds, offered blessings over animals, and sometimes resurrected deceased animals. He once persuaded a vicious wolf in the town of Gubbio, Italy, to stop terrorizing the neighborhood by negotiating a promise from the citizenry that they would treat the wolf kindly and make sure that it was fed. St. Francis is often represented with a variety of birds and animals at his side, including in particular a deer, a wolf, or a lamb.

See also pages 61 and 179.
See also page 199 for a Blessing of Animals.
See also pages 196–97 for St. Francis's "Canticle of the Sun".

St. Nicholas of Tolentino
Memorial: September 10

Born in 1295 in Sant'Angelo, Italy, and named after St. Nicholas of Myra, St. Nicholas was a devout youth who became an Augustinian friar at the age of eighteen, and was ordained at the age of twenty-five. He moved to the war-torn town of Tolentino at the beckoning of an angel. He performed many miracles there, which reportedly include the resurrection of over a hundred dead children. A strict vegetarian, he was once served a roasted partridge for dinner. Upon his making the sign of the cross over the bird, it sprang to life and flew out the window. Perhaps it is his refusal to consume animals or animal by-products that has made him a patron saint of animals. He is most well-known as the patron saint of the souls in purgatory. St. Nicholas died after a long illness in 1305 in Tolentino.

Pope St. Sylvester I
Memorial: December 31

St. Sylvester was a Roman citizen and a fourth-century pope during the time of Emperor Constantine I. St. Sylvester is said to have been responsible for the conversion of Constantine to Christianity. His patronage over domestic animals comes from his association with a bull he restored to life. As the story goes, St. Sylvester was debating a group of rabbis, one of whom was a magician. The magician, thinking to outwit his opponent, proclaimed that he knew the name of the Omnipotent and whispered the name into the bull's ear; some say he invoked the name of Satan instead. At that, the bull fell dead. St. Sylvester, recognizing the deed as evil, restored the bull to life by making the sign of the cross over it. He also founded and renovated many beautiful churches before his death in 335 in Rome. He is often represented artistically in the company of a bull.

For the General Protection of Livestock

St. Isidore the Farmer
Memorial: May 15

Born to poor and pious Catholic farmers in Spain around 1070, as a young child, St. Isidore was sent by his destitute parents to work for a wealthy landowner in Madrid. He worked the fields of that same estate throughout his life. He married Maria (Toribia) "de la Cabeza" (who, because her head was carried in a reliquary throughout the countryside following her death, became a saint invoked for rain). Together, they had one child, who died.

St. Isidore lived a simple, humble, holy life as a farm field hand, with most of his time spent plowing the fields. He was often found kneeling in prayer in the fields he plowed. He once arrived late to work, having lingered in prayer after morning Mass, which led to complaints from the other farmhands. The landowner reacted with a close observation of St. Isidore's work habits. He was surprised to see two angels guiding St. Isidore's plow whenever St. Isidore was absent, and when St. Isidore was working, the angels plowed beside him with white oxen, thereby doubling his productivity. The landowner never reprimanded St. Isidore. Later, the saint miraculously saved the life of the landowner's daughter.

St. Isidore had a profound concern for the treatment of animals, especially the oxen that drew the plows. He is said to have miraculously healed a horse that was dear to his employer. Other miracles attributed to him include the multiplication of food: once, for a flock of starving birds, and then again for a large group of beggars. St. Isidore died of a fever at the age of sixty. He was canonized in 1622. He is portrayed carrying a sickle and a sheaf of grain, sometimes with a white ox at his feet.

See also pages 62, 79, 152, and 165.
See also page 197 for a Prayer Invoking St. Isidore the Farmer.
See also page 215 for a Prayer for Rain.
See also page 218 for the Blessing of a Well.

For the Protection of Horned Livestock

St. Guy of Anderlecht
Memorial: September 12

Born near Brussels in 950, this humble farmer-turned-businessman, turned-pilgrim-and-church-sacristan, is said to have spent much of his life devoted to prayer, pilgrimages, and the care of the sick. He is frequently depicted in art and iconography as an ecclesiastic with an ox lying at his feet, as an angel is said to have regularly taken his place at an oxen-drawn plow in the field so that St. Guy could pray to God without distraction. He died in 1012 from a combination of exhaustion and natural causes.

See also pages 46 and 152.

For the Protection of Cattle

St. Bridget of Kildare
Memorial: February 1

This patroness of Ireland was born in Ulster around 451 to a Christian slave mother and a pagan father who kept a large herd of dairy cows. According to legend, a rare, white-colored, red-eared cow appeared daily to provide all the sustenance needed by the infant St. Bridget, which was interpreted as a sign that the child was marked for something special. From a young age she was given the daily responsibility of milking the cows and churning the milk into butter. One day, she gave away every bit of milk and butter to the poor. She was chastised and sent back into the pasture with instructions to not come home until she had recouped the day's losses. Sitting forlornly on her milking stool, she prayed for a sign that God was pleased with her generosity to the poor. A flight of angels carrying buckets, milking stools, and churns descended. Each of the angels took a seat beside a cow and began to milk. When the angels were finished, they produced three times as much butter as St. Bridget had given away.

Later in life, St. Bridget founded a double monastery, that is, a monastery for both monks and nuns, beneath a large oak tree, thereafter known as Kildara (in Gaelic, *Cill Dara*, or "Church of the Oak"), as well as other convents for nuns.

She is said to have sat at the bedside of her dying pagan father to weave the first St. Brigid's Cross from reeds. The cross is believed to protect both one's house and one's animals from evil and fire. According to tradition, a new St. Brigid's Cross was woven each year on her feast day, with the old one burned or tucked into the thatch of the roof, which was especially at risk from fire. St. Bridget died of natural causes in 523 in Kildare. She was buried at Downpatrick beside St. Patrick and St. Colmcille.

See also pages 67 and 90.

St. Kevin of Glendalough
Memorial: June 3

An Irish abbot and the founder of a monastery in Glendalough, near Dublin, Ireland, St. Kevin is the anglicized version of the name Coemgen, meaning "beautiful, shining birth." Kevin was born in 498, and legend states that a white cow appeared at the family's home every morning to provide milk for the infant. As a child, St. Kevin was said to have a short temper, a general dislike for people, and a great love for animals. He was educated by monks until he was twelve, then studied for the priesthood and eventually was ordained a bishop. Following his ordination, he frequently sought solitude in a hermit-like fashion, living in a mountainside cave that measured seven feet by three feet, which today is known as St. Kevin's Bed. There, he lived in close communion with the animals around him. Disciples sought him out as a teacher, which gave rise to the establishment of a seminary and several other monasteries in Glendalough. It was a cow that eventually inspired St. Kevin to return to active ministry. Every day when this particular cow was set out to pasture by his owner, a pagan farmer named Dima, the cow would climb the mountainside to lick the feet of St. Kevin as he knelt in prayer. When the cow returned each evening, she produced prolific amounts of milk—as much as the milk of fifty cows combined. The cow's owner, having grown curious, followed the cow all the way to the cave of St. Kevin. Upon seeing the cow lick the bishop's feet, the farmer fell to his knees in repentance. St. Kevin shared the gospel with Dima, who then begged the saint to come and teach his family as well. St. Kevin spent a day discerning God's will, after which he left the cave to share the gospel with many pagan families and followers of Christ in Glendalough and beyond. St. Kevin died in 618 and was canonized in 1903.

See also pages 64, 65, and 141–42.

The Four Crowned Martyrs
Sts. Castorius, Claudius, Nicostratus, and Simpronian
Memorial: November 8

These four Christian stonemasons were living and working in Pannoniam, now modern Hungary and parts of Austria, when they were commissioned by the Roman emperor Diocletian to carve a statue of the sun god in his chariot. After they had completed the statue, the emperor was so pleased, he commissioned them to carve other works. They were often seen making the sign of the cross over their tools and the stone they were chiseling. When their Christian beliefs led them to refuse to carve a statue of Asclepius, the Roman god of medicine, they were accused of sorcery and commanded to make a sacrifice to the sun god. They refused. They were beaten and whipped, then locked inside lead caskets that were thrown into the river.

While there does not seem to be a clear connection between cattle and these saints, it may be that cattle (oxen, as well as mules and horses) were their constant companions, since they would be essential in transporting the stonework. In Roman times, caravans of donkeys and mules were used for lighter loads. For heavier loads, oxen were yoked together to pull the weight of the stone. It took about twelve pairs of oxen to pull a ten-ton load. However, if even one animal broke down, the entire operation would come to a grinding halt. As the number of oxen increased, the probability of breakdown became higher. Thus, it may be surmised that as craftsmen and as Christians, they would have treated these beasts of burden with the utmost care and respect.

St. Cunera
Memorial: June 12

According to legend, St. Cunera was a fourth-century British princess as well as one of the holy virgins who accompanied St. Ursula on a pilgrimage to Rome. On their return trip home, the entire group of pilgrims was attacked by Huns. St. Cunera alone was spared from the massacre through the intercession of a Frisian king, Radbod, who with great compassion took her into his castle in Rhenen, located in the modern Netherlands. At his kind bidding, she helped to run the royal household and immersed herself in a life of prayer and good works, especially tending to the poor. Nevertheless, perhaps because of her beauty, she became the target of the queen. In a fit of jealousy, the queen had Cunera strangled by one of her royal attendants while the king was on a hunting trip. The body was buried hastily in a cattle shed. When the king returned, the king's horse balked at being stabled in the shed where the body was interred. When the king inquired as to the whereabouts of Cunera, he was told her parents had come to take their daughter home. That same evening, mysterious lights formed the sign of a cross over St. Cunera's burial site, which led the king to discover the treachery. He flew into a rage and accused his wife of the murder. It is said the queen's guilt and her fear of the king's punishment drove her mad.

St. Cunera is widely venerated in Utrecht, where a church with an imposing tower was built at Rhenen directly over the place where she suffered martyrdom. Sick people flocked to the site seeking and receiving cures through her intercession. People also brought diseased cattle to the holy site in the hopes that their cattle would receive miraculous healings.

St. Gunthildis of Suffersheim
Memorial: September 22

A milkmaid known for her Christian charity and love for the poor, St. Gunthildis lived in Bavaria, Germany, in the mid-eleventh century. During prayer she was led to two crystal-clear springs where both she and the cattle under her care obtained good health. It is said the cows that drank from the springs gave copious amounts of milk, such that no one who was poor went without. Legend has it that her employer confronted her just as she was about to give a bucket of milk to the poor. She said it was a bucket of lye. He peered into the bucket, and indeed it was filled with lye.

St. Gunthildis died of natural causes in 1057. She was so beloved by the cattle in her care, it is said her burial site was chosen by the oxen who refused to budge when they reached a particularly beautiful spot in Suffersheim. A chapel was built over her grave, and many miracles have been reported at that site. She is depicted in art and iconography with a bucket of milk, or holding cheese, and with a cow at her side.

St. Perpetua
Memorial: March 7

In the year 203, at the age of twenty-two, Vivia Perpetua, a noblewoman from Carthage, became a Christian. Under the persecution of the Roman emperor Severus, she, along with four other catechumens, including a young pregnant woman named Felicity, were arrested. Perpetua was baptized just before being taken to prison. Having already borne a child and likely a widow, St. Perpetua was separated from her baby, then mercifully reunited with the child in prison until the time of her martyrdom. Despite her family's pleas and her love for her child, she refused to recant her Christian beliefs.

On the day of their martyrdom in March of 203, Sts. Perpetua and Felicity were stripped and covered in nets, then sent into an arena to be killed by a mad cow. As bloodthirsty as the crowd was, they felt the two women should not be humiliated in this manner. They were taken out of the arena and given tunics to wear. They then returned to the arena with the cow. The two stayed close to each other as they awaited the attack. They were thrown to the ground by the cow and were severely injured but not killed. Once again, the crowd protested the brutality, so the two saints were instead slain by the swords of gladiators.

Patrons of Barn Cats and Farm Dogs

What farm is complete without an intrepid farm dog or two, as well as a couple of barn cats who keep the vermin in check? Here are a few saints you can call on to be a dog's or cat's spiritual best friend.

For the Protection of Barn Cats

St. Gertrude of Nivelles
Memorial: March 17

An unofficial but widely invoked saint of all things feline, St. Gertrude of Nivelles's affinity with cats likely has more to do with her official status as a patroness against vermin. This didn't happen immediately, but some say it began in the 1980s with a catchy catalog, *Metropolitan Cats*, published by the Metropolitan Museum of Art in New York. The catalog featured St. Gertrude, the abbess of a seventh-century Benedictine monastery in what is now Belgium, in the company of a cat. Modern readers pegged her as a cat person and the association was established. Her traditional representation in art and statuary with mice climbing up her staff (the creatures were said to symbolize the souls in purgatory, for whom she interceded with great devotion) as well as tales of banishing mice from the farmers' fields with her prayers, served to solidify her title as a holy cat lady.

See also pages 13 and 107.

Bl. Julian of Norwich
Memorial: May 13

Bl. Julian of Norwich was a fourteenth-century English mystic and anchoress who, in 1373, voluntarily confined herself to a cell, or anchor hold, attached to a Norwich parish. In that cell, in the sole company of her beloved cat, with whom she is most often depicted, she devoted herself to prayer and contemplation on behalf of the needs of the church, the citizens of Norwich, and the whole world. Around the year 1393, Bl. Julian wrote a text called *Revelations of Divine Love*, which elaborated on her understanding of the sixteen mystical visions ("showings") of Christ's passion that were revealed to her in the throes of her own near-fatal illness twenty years earlier. These visions led her to an even deeper contemplation of and appreciation for Christ's unfathomable love.

Despite having Our Lord, vowing never to leave her cell certainly ensured that Bl. Julian would experience loneliness. While she acted as a spiritual advisor to many people from behind the curtained window of her cell, one may surmise it was her own dear animal companion that provided tangible love and tactile comfort throughout years spent in deep prayer. Perhaps her nameless yet famous cat was also her daily partner in prayer. It may also have been this human-animal bond that helped to anchor Bl. Julian in the love, goodness, and joy of the natural world. She died in 1416 of natural causes.

Interestingly, a written rule existed stating that anchoresses could keep no pets other than cats, reflecting a belief that cats were the creatures best suited to an atmosphere of prayer, holy silence, and contemplation. Specifically, a thirteenth-century rule for anchoresses known as the *Ancrene Riwle* stated, "You shall not possess any beast, my dear sisters, except for a cat."

St. Philip Neri
Memorial: May 26

Another patron of cats is the sixteenth-century Italian saint known as the Apostle of Rome. Renowned for his cheerfulness and devotion, St. Philip Neri went about his priestly duties with a special devotion to the poor of Rome, carrying his pet cat in a basket. He constructed an oratory over the church of San Girolamo, in Rome, where he lived in a cell with his cat, whom he employed in the transformation of proud nobles into humble saints. As a penance for their sins, he would often require penitents to feed or carry his cat around, a gentle way of humbling the rich as well as his own disciples, none of whom were above caring for his animal companion. When he was asked by the pope to relocate to a monastery in Vallicella, he left his beloved cat behind in the care of the monks at the oratory as an example of self-sacrifice, though he made frequent inquiries as to her well-being and continued to oversee her care from afar. The cat lived for six more years and is said to have become one of the most beloved and celebrated personalities in Rome. According to a famous eighteenth-century poem by English poet Christopher Smart, the cat's given name was Jeoffry, though other sources maintain that the cat was a female. St. Philip Neri died in 1595 on the Feast of Corpus Christi of natural causes after suffering a series of illnesses, each of which had been cured by prayer alone.

For the Protection of Farm Dogs

St. Hubert of Liège
Memorial: November 3

St. Hubert was a priest and later the bishop of Liège who, throughout the late seventh and early eighth centuries, evangelized the Ardennes region of France. Long known as a patron saint of hunters and trappers, he was also invoked against rabies and bad behavior in dogs, particularly hunting dogs, from as early as the ninth century. (Bloodhounds are also known as St. Hubert's hounds.) With rabies reaching epidemic proportions at that time, it was customary to brand the skin of dogs with a white-hot Key of St. Hubert, proclaimed in the Ardennes region of France as a preventative strategy so that dogs would not contract the disease, or, in cases where a dog had been bitten by a rabid animal, the key was heated and pressed to the bite wound as a means of sterilization, cauterization, and healing. Such keys were used primarily by priests and religious in locations where St. Hubert had established some sort of connection during his lifetime. The key itself was a piece of iron, often forged into the shape of a cross or a cone sacramental, but the effectiveness of it hinged on the faith of the user. It was dispensed in great numbers as late as the 1870s by Benedictine monks living at the abbey where St. Hubert's relics were kept. The keys were hung on the walls of houses as protection against rabies for residents and their beloved dogs. St. Hubert died in 727 of natural causes as he was praying the Our Father.

See also pages 19–20.

St. Roch
Memorial: August 16

According to writers of his *Acta* (life story), St. Roch (also known as St. Rocco), was born in Montpellier, France, around the year 1295. He was the privileged son of the governor of Montpellier and his wife, both of whom died before St. Roch's twentieth birthday. On his father's deathbed, St. Roch received the governorship of Montpellier, which he promptly transferred to his uncle. He then sold all his worldly goods for the benefit of the needy and undertook a pilgrimage to Rome for the purpose of ministering to the poor and sick. His plan seemed to have met with divine approval, for he was granted the gift of healing. This gift became most evident when St. Roch passed through an area north of Rome where the townspeople were suffering from the bubonic plague. He not only nursed the sick but also miraculously cured a great many when he made the sign of the cross over their afflicted bodies. He remained for some time in Rome, where the plague had spread, caring for and curing the afflicted, including the brother of the pope.

St. Roch traveled extensively, bringing his gift of healing to plague-infected towns and their despairing citizens as well as to ailing animals. He is known to have cured cattle by marking their heads with the sign of the cross. It is said that in the city of Piacenza, St. Roch himself contracted the plague. Unwilling to be a burden to others, he withdrew into the forest to die. Before long, however, he was miraculously befriended by a dog, who daily licked his sores and brought him a share of bread from his master's table, which provided him enough sustenance to survive. One day, the nobleman to whom the dog belonged followed his hunting companion into the woods and discovered the ailing St. Roch, whom he took into his home until his recovery was complete.

In gratitude, St. Roch returned to the city of Piacenza and cured many more people and livestock by imparting over them his blessing and the sign of the cross. Eventually, he returned to Montpellier, where, now unrecognizable, so aged and transformed by his sickness had he become, he was arrested, allegedly on his uncle's orders, on suspicion of being a spy, and was thrown into prison. Unwilling to call attention to his own noble birth, he remained in prison where he was ministered to by an angel of God until his natural death in 1327. It was only then that the unique birthmark on his chest in the shape of a red cross revealed him as the miracle worker who, by the grace of God, had saved so many from the hands of the Black Death. In 1485, the relics of St. Roch were enshrined in the church of San Rocco, Venice, where they remain to this day. He is frequently depicted in art as a pilgrim with a dog at his feet, with a dog licking a plague sore, or with a dog carrying a loaf of bread in its mouth.

———

Patrons of Horses and Donkeys

A mainstay of farming, a horse may be employed in plowing fields, rounding up other livestock, pulling a cart or buggy, or providing transportation. A horse may also serve as a trusty steed for trail riding or in equestrian sports, family companion, pretty pasture puff, or precious pet of a little girl whose first love is the pony in the barn. A donkey typically provides comic relief, a strong back for packing, plowing, or carting, and, given its territorial nature, swift kicks, and screeching brays, can act as a fierce guardian against predators. Throughout the ages, these versatile equines have been as essential to farm life as sunlight and rain.

For the Protection of Horses

St. Coloman of Stockerau
Memorial: October 13

Son of an Irish king, St. Coloman, a monk, set off on a pilgrimage to the Holy Land in 1012 by way of the north side of the Danube. There was intense fighting throughout that region, and when his horse lost a shoe and St. Coloman sought the services of a local blacksmith, his foreign garb and inability to speak German gave rise to accusations that he was a spy. He was arrested and hanged from an elder tree at Stockerau near Vienna, Austria. His incorrupt body was buried at Melk, the Austrian seat of power at the time.

His pilgrimage had brought him through the village of Schwangau, Germany. There, on the second Sunday of October, an annual feast dating to the sixteenth century known as Colomansfest takes place. More than two hundred horses and their Bavarian-costumed riders proceed to St. Coloman's Church, where an outdoor Mass is celebrated by a priest on horseback, and all the horses are blessed. Afterward, an event known as Coloman's Ride takes place, whereby St. Coloman's relic is displayed and honored as clergy and guests of honor circle the church twice in horse-drawn, decorated carriages. Also on his feast day, there is in Melk a blessing that invokes St. Coloman's powerful intercession asking for the protection and healing of horses and cattle.

St. Eligius of Noyon
Memorial: December 1

Owing to his earliest beginnings as a farrier, St. Eligius is best known for his patronage of horses. A summer festival in Provence, France, held in his name, takes place each year on June 25. On that day, local farmers dress their horses, donkeys, and mules in festival harnesses and parade to the chapel or into the center of town to receive from the local priests an annual blessing for health and an invocation for the protection of St. Eligius.

See also pages 23–24, 99, 101, and 132.

St. George
Memorial: April 23

Born in the late second century and raised by his widowed mother, St. George was a devout Christian who enlisted in the Roman army at the age of seventeen and rose through the military ranks to become a member of the Roman emperor Diocletian's Praetorian Guard. When St. George confessed his faith and refused to take part in Diocletian's persecution of Christians, he was subject to a series of merciless tortures that miraculously failed to harm or weaken him. St. George was beheaded in 303 at Lydda, Palestine.

His display of Christian courage and holy resistance during his lifetime converted many witnesses, including Diocletian's own wife, the Empress Alexandria, who was also martyred for her faith. A few years later, when Constantine became the emperor of the Roman Empire, St. George's relics were venerated at a church in Lydda that was dedicated to him. He became known as the Great Martyr and many miracles are attributed to him.

The most famous legend attributed to St. George is his slaying of a large serpent, or dragon, who lived in a lake near the town of Silena, in Libya. The ferocious beast prevented the townspeople from drawing water from the lake.

In an effort to appease the dragon, they first offered it a diet of sheep. When the dragon was not appeased, they offered it young virgins, chosen by lots, in conformity with their pagan beliefs. One day, the king's own daughter was chosen to be sacrificed. She was standing on the banks of the lake about to be eaten by the dragon when St. George, armed with a spear and shield, rode in on a magnificent white horse. He made the sign of the cross, pinned the dragon to the ground with his spear, and the mighty steed trampled the serpent beneath its hooves. St. George bade the king's daughter to leash the neck of the dragon with her belt. The dragon was led back to Silena, where the dragon was slain by the sword of St. George. St. George is most often portrayed as mounted upon a white horse, although Eastern Orthodox iconography permits him to ride a black horse.

In Germanic lore, St. George's dragon terrorized a little town known as Ebringen, located in the foothills of the Black Forest. The winged dragon, who resided in a mountainside cave instead of a lake, was similarly dispatched by the chivalrous saint. In commemoration, the villagers of Ebringen mounted stone crosses on the peaks of their houses. Until recently, an annual festival was held there every April 23, at which time the local farmers and villagers would ride their horses around the church three times, invoking St. George's protection for their horses.

See also page 56.

St. Giles
Memorial: September 1

St. Giles was the wonder-working child of a wealthy Greek family who from an early age demonstrated a deep love of nature and all God's creatures. He donated his inheritance to the poor and became a hermit who lived in a cave in southern France that was obstructed by a thick thornbush. A white deer nourished and sustained the hermit with her milk, and became his beloved companion. One day, when the king of the Goths was out hunting, he pursued the white deer to the mouth of the cave. The king shot an arrow at the doe, but it struck St. Giles instead. The king was overcome with remorse for having wounded the holy man. In recompense, he gifted St. Giles with a plot of land for the building of a monastery. Seeing the event as the will of God, St. Giles left the cave and founded a Benedictine monastery, where he became highly regarded for his holiness, wisdom, and the working of miracles.

St. Giles's association with horses stems from the king's appearance on horseback, which he interpreted as a revelation of God's will for his life. Also of note is that many of the 162 churches built in his honor throughout France, Britain, Belgium, Germany, Italy, and the Czech Republic were built near crossroads, where travelers could stop to pray while their horses were being rested, reshod, and refreshed and, naturally, prayed for too. St. Giles, who is one of the Fourteen Holy Helpers, died in 721 of natural causes.

See also page 55.

St. Guy of Anderlecht
Memorial: September 12

St. Guy's grave was nearly forgotten until a horse revealed its location by deliberately coming to a halt right above it. An early devotee of the saint was said to have hired two boys to install hedges around the gravesite to protect it from being accidentally trampled. The boys mocked their employer's concern for the dead and, upon doing so, were seized with horrible stomach pains, and died. This inspired the locals to make pilgrimages to his grave and to eventually build an oratory on the site. In 1076, a church was constructed and dedicated to St. Guy. As late as 1914, pilgrimages to Anderlecht by cab drivers and their horses were made annually. Farmers, grooms, and stablemen, along with their animals, also came there to be blessed.

See also pages 32 and 152.

St. Hippolytus of Rome
Memorial: August 13

A Roman soldier in the third century, St. Hippolytus was assigned to guard Christian prisoners who were being persecuted for their faith. In the course of his duties, he was converted by their steadfast witness as well as by St.

Lawrence in particular, whose body he buried. Afterward, when confronted by the emperor, he made a public profession of his faith. He was beaten, then dragged by wild horses through the streets just outside Rome to a death by dismemberment. This was thought to be an ironic manner of punishment meted out by the Roman prefect, given that the name *Hippolytus* means "a horse turned loose" or "unleasher of horses." It was also the name of the Hippolytus of Greek mythology, who was executed in the same violent manner—a story likely known to his pagan persecutors.

During the Middle Ages, sick horses were brought to St. Ippolyts, a church in Hertfordshire, England, named after St. Hippolytus, where their owners sought the healing intercession of this heroic saint.

St. Leonard of Noblac
Memorial: November 6
St. Leonard was a Frankish noble in the fifth-century court of Clovis I, and, later, a pious hermit who performed miracles and lived in the forest near Limoges. St. Leonard petitioned Clovis I for the right to liberate prisoners at will, at any time. His request was granted, and St. Leonard secured the freedom of many. To some of these he gave a portion of the vast, forested land in Noblat (located in the Limousin region of France) that had been granted to him by royal decree for the building of a monastery. This land allowed the former prisoners a fresh start farming the land and making a decent living. It is said that prisoners who prayerfully invoked him from their cells were astonished when their chains broke apart right before their very eyes. Afterward, they would seek out the saint with their iron chains in tow and offer their gratitude and discipleship. During his lifetime and continuing after his death in 559, St. Leonard was revered as an advocate of prisoners as well as the mentally ill, who until the eighteenth century typically were shackled in chains. However, over time, especially in the region of Bavaria and Germany, the chains with which he was associated became connected with livestock chains, and St. Leonard became known as a patron of all farm animals, especially of horses, stalls, and stables.

Churches and chapels dedicated to St. Leonard proliferated throughout the area. Today, they are seats of annual Leonhardi celebrations that take place in mid-October. Men, women, and children mounted on ornately decorated horses proceed to the church or chapel and circle it three times. The priest confers a blessing on the horses and other livestock, and then the church or chapel is encircled with a chain in honor of St. Leonard. Links or sections of iron chains are often left by pilgrims throughout the year in his honor and in gratitude for prayers answered through his intercession.

A Bavarian blessing of protection goes like this: *Gott, wird Euch geben, Glück und Segen, in Haus und Stall und Überall! Bei Pferd und Rind, bei Schaf und Schwein da soll Euer heiliger Leonhard sein!* Roughly translated, it means "May God give you happiness and blessing in your home and barn and everywhere! By your horse and cattle, by your sheep and pigs, there shall your Saint Leonhard be!"

See also page 79.

St. Martin of Tours
Memorial: November 12

As a young man following in the footsteps of his father (who was a senior officer in the Imperial Horse Guard stationed in northern Italy), St. Martin became an elite cavalry officer in the Roman Imperial Army at Milan in the fourth century. During a night patrol, which St. Martin conducted on horseback, a poor, nearly naked man appeared before him. Using his sword, St. Martin cut his warm military cloak in half so that he could share it with the poor man. The next night, the same man appeared to St. Martin in a dream, and revealed that he was Jesus. It is said that Martin's cloak was then restored to wholeness. The image of St. Martin riding his horse and meeting Christ as a beggar has been immortalized through the ages by artists and iconographers, giving rise to the saint's patronage of horses and therefore of equestrians as well. Upon his release from military service, St. Martin declared his vocation and became a monk, a priest, and subsequently the beloved bishop of Tours. He died in 397 of natural causes.

In many Spanish-speaking nations, St. Martin is popularly known as *San Martín Caballero* (meaning a gentleman knight who necessarily would have excelled at riding on horseback). He is also associated in Latin American countries with bringing good luck, because the faithful believe the horse St. Martin rode produced the first lucky horseshoe.

See also pages 66 and 120.

St. Stephen
Memorial: December 26

The first feast day following Christmas fittingly honors the saint who was one of the first deacons of the early church and, most significantly, the first martyr for Christ. As a Greek-speaking Jew, St. Stephen was a well-versed and eloquent orator who inspired many conversions. His effective Christian witness drew the attention and ire of the chief priests and elders of the temple. He was put on trial for blasphemy, then stoned to death in 36 for proclaiming before the Sanhedrin court his beatific vision of the risen Christ with God.

A tenth-century German poem recounts how St. Stephen was converted when Jesus miraculously cured the saint's own sick horse. Other explanations for his patronage of horses abound: On the day after Christmas, St. Stephen's feast day, horses were traditionally galloped at a frantic pace to increase their circulation, then were cut by a farrier, and bled out just enough to ensure good health over the winter. Another tradition in pre-Christian Germanic regions held that horses were sacrificed at Christmastime. In medieval times, the period of "Twelfth Night," which encompasses the feast of St. Stephen, was an appointed time of rest for domestic animals, chief among them the horse, which was particularly honored for its usefulness to the farmer. Lastly, legend states that St. Stephen tamed a wild horse simply by showing it a cross. Throughout Europe, horses, along with water and salt (to be used in times of sickness), oats, and hay, are customarily blessed on St. Stephen's feast day. The horses are then paraded around the churchyard, circling the church three times. In Ireland, such festivities include young boys racing around on stick horses that recalled the "Hobbies"—the ancient horses of the Celts—giving rise to the modern "hobby horse." Villagers bake bread in the shape of horseshoes (St. Stephen's Horns, or *podkovy*), and horses are harnessed to sleighs to provide a fun ride through the countryside known as St. Stephen's Ride.

St. Teilo of Llandaff
Memorial: February 9

Born to a noble Welsh family in the late fifth century, St. Teilo founded a monastery in Dyfed, Wales, and became the bishop of Llandaff in 495. Little is known about his life, but he was a contemporary of St. David, the patron saint of Wales, who may have been his cousin. He and St. David made a pilgrimage to Jerusalem, where St. Teilo was consecrated a bishop. In 567, when Wales was struck by the yellow plague, St. Teilo fled to Brittany, where he lived for seven years. He is often depicted riding on a stag, owing to a legend that when a local nobleman in Brittany offered St. Teilo all the land he could encircle between sunset and sunrise, St. Teilo selected a stag to ride so that he could cover as much ground as possible. Perhaps his bareback ride on the legendary stag created his association with horses.

An alternate source of his connection to horses might be another legend that took place during his exile to Brittany. When, by the grace of God, the yellow plague departed from the whole isle of Britain, St. Teilo called his exiled followers from every country to return home with him. The ruler of the district, King Budic, met him with a large army of Armoricans, begging his help to vanquish a huge viper, or dragon, that had already destroyed a third of his kingdom. St. Teilo agreed only after receiving the urging of an angel as well as the promise of Christ's protection. He succeeded in vanquishing the dragon to the sea. However, fearing it would return, the king begged St. Teilo to remain there among them. Once again, God's will was communicated to the saint by an angel, who proclaimed that as a sign God wished him to stay, King Budic would appear with his army and offer him one of his best horses to ride back to Dól to assume the bishopric there. But, the angel cautioned, the saint was to refuse the horse, as he would receive "a most excellent steed sent to thee from God through me." The following day, the king and his army converged upon the saint, just as the angel had foretold. St. Teilo refused the king's horse, whereupon there appeared to him "a most beautiful steed, sent by God to him." He mounted God's horse and rode to Dól, where he remained for some time. When he departed from Dól, he called King Budic to him, blessed him, gave him the God-sent horse, and prayed in the presence of all that the soldiers of Armorica might excel in horsemanship and thereby defend their country. It is said that according to historical accounts, the Armorican soldiers were seven times more valiant as horsemen than as foot soldiers.

St. Vincent de Paul
Memorial: September 27

The son of a poor peasant family, St. Vincent de Paul was born in the village of Puoy, France, in 1581. He was educated at an early age by Franciscan friars and aspired to escape his lowly station as a farmer by becoming a priest. He became increasingly ashamed of his family and their farm, where he had worked long hours tending cattle, sheep, horses, cows, and pigs. He went off to the seminary, where he refused visits from his father, whose shabby clothing and limping gait caused him embarrassment.

St. Vincent became a priest at the age of nineteen. Charming and likeable, he was well received by the religious elite. One such admirer was an elderly woman from Toulouse, who left him a small inheritance, which he had to travel some distance to claim. Needing the money to pay off some prior debts, he hired a horse and set out on the journey, only to find that the man in possession of the inheritance had fled to Marseilles, where he reportedly was living in grand style. St. Vincent had no money to pursue the crook, so he himself became one, illegally selling his hired horse with the intention of paying for it upon his return. He found the scoundrel, had him thrown into prison, and claimed roughly three hundred crowns. On his return, he was beset by a series of misfortunes. He was sold into slavery and remained a slave for two years. He made a pact with God that if he would spare his life and set him free, he would devote the remainder of his life to the service of the poor. True to his word, upon attaining his freedom, he established confraternities of charity for the physically, spiritually, and materially poor and sick.

He founded hospitals, ransomed thousands of galley slaves from North Africa, implemented much-needed reforms in the training and education of seminarians, and conducted retreats for the clergy. Having been an excellent rider from his youth, he traversed much of the countryside on horseback. In his elderly years, consistent with his humble spirit, he rode an old horse that was as worn and willing as he was, until at last he could ride no more. He died of natural causes in Paris, France, in 1660.

It has been reported that St. Vincent wrote more than thirty thousand letters in his lifetime, nearly seven thousand of which were collected in the eighteenth century. Many of these letters reflect his extensive knowledge of horses, using terminology and analogies specific to equestrian activities and referencing dramatic experiences of being kicked by a horse and falling under a horse.

For the Protection of Pack Horses

St. Blaise
Memorial: February 3
Tradition has it that as St. Blaise was being led down the mountain to his death by his captors, he stopped to bless each and every draft horse he passed along the way. The blessing of draft horses is a time-honored annual Bavarian tradition that takes place on February 3, the feast day of St. Blaise, when farmers bring their packhorses to church to be blessed by the parish priest. In some areas, the horses wore a small brass comb behind one ear in a nod to the way St. Blaise was tortured and martyred, which was by having his flesh torn to bits with sharp iron combs like those used in the preparation of wool for weaving.

See also pages 5, 59, 101, and 126.

For the Protection of Donkeys

St. Anthony of Padua
Memorial: June 13

Legend states that St. Anthony made a wager with a skeptical merchant in Rimini, Italy, about the real presence of Christ in the Eucharist. He bet the skeptic that the man's donkey, if starved for three days, would still prefer the Eucharist to a pail of food. St. Anthony won the bet, and the merchant was converted. In a variation of this story, a local heretic stated he would not believe in the real presence unless a horse would kneel before the Blessed Sacrament. After praying, St. Anthony held the Eucharist in one hand and oats in the other in front of a horse, which turned away from the oats and knelt before the Blessed Sacrament. The heretic became a Christian.

See also pages 27–28, 58, and 144.
See also page 197 for the Prayer of St. Anthony.
See also page 203 for the Prayer to St. Anthony for Lost Animals.

For Protection against Horse Theft

St. Castulus of Rome
Memorial: March 26

St. Castulus's feast day in early spring, which coincides with planting time, inspired the devotion of farmers and shepherds. Since farmers relied heavily on draft horses to prepare and plow their planting fields, naturally they would have concerns about their valuable equine assets being stolen. St. Castulus's patronage against horse theft may be rooted in the transportation of his relics in the eighth century to Moosburg, Bavaria, an area historically known for trade between the Bavarians and the Slavs of horses and other commodities.

Where there are horse traders, there is horse theft, and the local laws reflected the high value of horses. A holy helper such as St. Castulus would have provided farmers with blessed assurance that their horses would remain safe and sound in the barn.

See also page 188.

See also page 188.

Patrons of Rams, Sheep, and Swine

Raised for food, breeding, fiber, or dairy products, these profitable livestock are protected by patron saints who stand ready to intercede for the animal's health as well as for the farmer's wealth.

For the Protection of Rams

St. Giles
Memorial: September 1

St. Giles's affinity for creatures of all species likely led pilgrims to associate him with the animals they themselves held most dear. Long ago, on his feast day in Spain, rams were bathed, their wool was dyed in bright colors, and they were paraded down the mountainsides to village churches, where they received a blessing. In the Pyrenees mountains in the Basque region, costumed shepherds bring their prized rams down the mountainsides and honor St. Giles on his feast day by praying the Mass.

See also pages 45–46.

For the Protection of Sheep and Lambs

St. Drogo
Memorial: April 16

Born of Flemish nobility, St. Drogo's childhood was marked by deep guilt over his mother's death during his birth. At the age of eighteen and following his father's death, he disposed of all his worldly goods and became a pilgrim who served Christ in utter poverty and penance. He journeyed to Rome nine times.

He hired himself out for more than twenty years to tend cattle and sheep on the estate of a wealthy, pious landowner in the village of Sebourg, which bordered Belgium and France. He aspired to become a good shepherd after the model of Christ, and to learn all that he could about the needs of the flocks he tended. Over time, he gained a reputation as a master of shepherding. Known to use bilocation, he was often seen both working in the field or tending his flock at the same time as he was attending Mass.

He died in 1186 at the age of eighty-four. On his feast day, in the region where he lived and worked, he is invoked for the protection of sheep and their farmers at an annual Shepherd's Mass.

St. George
Memorial: April 23

The most famous legend attributed to St. George is his slaying of a large serpent, or dragon, that lived in a lake near the town of Silena, Libya. Having exhausted their supply of sheep, the townspeople offered it a steady diet of young virgins, chosen by lots, in the hopes of appeasing the dragon. Of course, St. George not only slew the dragon and saved the king's own daughter as well as future generations of young women but also presumably saved generations of new flocks of sheep from being eaten by a fire-breathing dragon. This legend has endeared St. George to shepherds and shepherdesses throughout the ages. These days, a blessing of the sheep takes place on St. George's feast day in many communities all over the world. In a Cretan village called Asi Gonia shepherds gather their flocks in the courtyard of St. George Galata (St. George the Milkman) to receive a blessing from an Orthodox priest. The sheep are then milked, and the buckets of fresh, sweet milk are bottled and offered for sale to the crowd by milkmaids dressed in colorful, traditional costumes.

See also pages 44–45.

St. John the Baptist
Memorial: June 24

The cousin of Jesus, and the son of Zechariah and his once-barren wife Elizabeth, St. John the Baptist was a prophet and forerunner of Christ. While living an ascetic life in the wilderness, he preached a fiery message of repentance and performed baptisms in the Jordan River. Most significantly, he baptized Jesus, whom St. John acknowledged by exclaiming, "Behold, the Lamb of God" (John 1:36). St. John was later arrested and executed at the command of King Herod, who bowed to his bitter wife's demand for the head of the Baptist, whose chastisements had offended her. Given that the lamb is the most common attribute of St. John the Baptist (a symbol of his recognition of Jesus as "the Lamb of God"), he naturally became associated with the protection of lambs.

For the Protection of Swine and Pigs

St. Anthony the Abbot
Memorial: January 17
Born in Egypt in 251 to a wealthy family, St. Anthony was orphaned at the age of twenty, when he decided to give all his worldly possessions to the poor. Considered the Father of Monks, St. Anthony founded the first Christian monastery in Palestine, which, centuries later, served as a model for St. Benedict. St. Anthony lived both as a hermit in a rock-hewn tomb in the desert and, later, in the ruins of a mountaintop fort, where he observed long periods of fasting and penance. A strict vegetarian, he did not see any human being but the man who brought him bread every six months for twenty long years. He died of natural causes in 356.

The saint is often depicted in Christian art with a pig, which some say signifies the devil who assailed him constantly in his eremitical life; others maintain it represents a pig he miraculously healed. In any case, St. Anthony the Abbot's connection with pigs chiefly relates to his curing of people stricken with "St. Anthony's Fire." This affliction is identified as either modern-day shingles, of which he is also the patron saint, or ergotism, which was prevalent in the Middle Ages. Ergotism resulted from consuming a fungus that contaminated rye flour. People stricken with the disease often suffered from gangrene, which felt like a fire blazing all over the skin. St. Anthony is said to have prepared an ointment, derived from the fat of pigs, with which he anointed and miraculously healed people stricken with ergotism. During the Middle Ages, Germans in every village set aside a pig that would be donated to the monks running the local hospital for this very purpose. Some traditions held that where a blessing of animals took place on St. Anthony the Abbot's feast day, farmers must save from slaughter one piglet coming from every litter so that this pig would be blessed at church. This gave rise to the expression, "to come back more times than the pig of St. Anthony."

See also pages 28–29, 86, and 96.

St. Anthony of Padua
Memorial: June 13

Born in 1195, St. Anthony turned his back on the prestige and advantages of his wealthy family, choosing instead a cloistered lifestyle of humility. St. Anthony became widely known for his gifts of preaching and teaching. He was courageous as an evangelist, traveling first to Morocco and then throughout northern Italy and France. He died in 1231 of natural causes and was buried in Padua.

The timing of the saint's feast day coincides with the time of year when farmers typically sell their first piglings of the season. Another loose association can be derived from the fact that during the time that he lived as a hermit, St. Anthony frequently ate the roots of plants, which was the same diet as the wild boars that roamed all about him. At least one remote village in Spain still recognizes St. Anthony of Padua's feast day annually by setting loose a pig with a bell around its neck. The Pig of St. Anthony is permitted to freely roam the streets for six months as a local celebrity and spoiled community pet. However, its liberty and state of privileged indulgence end abruptly on January 17, the feast day of St. Anthony the Abbot, when the pig is given for their sustenance to the poorest family in the village. In modern times, the pig is raffled off to the highest bidder, and the proceeds are donated to a local nonprofit.

See also pages 27–28, 53, and 144.
See also page 197 for the Prayer of St. Anthony.
See also page 203 for the Prayer to St. Anthony for Lost Animals.

St. Blaise
Memorial: February 3

During the persecution of Christians by the Roman emperor Licinius, St. Blaise fled to a cave outside the city. There, he lived in solitude until a group of hunters who were gathering wild beasts to devour Christians in the amphitheater happened upon the hermit in his cave. He was seized and forced-marched down the mountainside toward prison. Along the way, the group encountered a woman whose pig was being carried off by a wolf. To the astonishment of everyone, St. Blaise commanded the wolf to release the pig, which the wolf did, and the pig was freed unharmed. It did not end so well for St. Blaise, however, who was tortured and beheaded sometime around the year 316. He is one of the Fourteen Holy Helpers whose intercession is considered especially powerful, so much so that many modern-day swineherds carve the name of St. Blaise on their staves.

See also pages 5, 52, 101, and 126.

For the Protection of Hares and Other Small Creatures

St. Melangell
Memorial: May 27

Whether farming rabbits, or working to ensure that rabbits and other small animals vacate your vegetable gardens or fields, there's one saint who outperforms others by leaps and bounds: St. Melangell. St. Melangell was a devout, sixth-century Irish princess who defied her father's wish that she should marry. Instead, she fled to the wilderness outside the Tanat Valley in Northern Wales. She took refuge in a cave, living on nuts and berries and keeping company with various small creatures.

Approximately fifteen years into her solitary confinement, the Prince of Powys (Wales), together with his pack of hounds, went hare hunting in the Derwyn Hills. Following the baying of his hounds, he gave chase to a hare that darted into a thicket, eventually taking refuge in the folds of St. Melangell's garments. The fervent hounds became docile and quiet in the presence of the peaceful woman. The king, quite intrigued, dismounted and listened to her sad tale of escape and exile from her homeland in Ireland. He was so impressed with her piety and beauty that he asked for her hand in marriage. When she refused, he donated a portion of land that she might use in service to God. The saint lived in a small cell built upon the land that came to be known as Pennant Melangell. She also founded a monastery there and remained protective of the docile hares (known as Melangell's lambs) and other small animals with whom she coexisted until her death thirty-seven years later, in 590. A church was built over her cell and remains a place of peaceful contemplation and sanctuary as well as a place of worship for the local farming community. Thanks to St. Melangell's intercession, hares are protected throughout the parish boundaries even today. She is considered the patron saint of animals in Wales, and is the patron saint of hares, small creatures, and the natural environment.

———

Patrons of Birds of the Air

*From swallows, barn owls, doves, and blackbirds, to chickens,
geese, sparrows, and hawks, birds of every feather can be found
around the farm. Whether these birds are welcome or
unwelcome, there are patron saints whose prayers have wings.*

For the General Protection of Birds

St. Francis of Assisi
Memorial: October 4

Born in Assisi, Italy, in 1181 to a wealthy family, Francesco Bernadone experienced a deep conversion in his early twenties and renounced all his worldly goods and status to become a poor itinerant preacher of the gospel.

Once, while journeying with his brethren through the Spoleto Valley, St. Francis came upon an enormous flock of birds of many varieties. He left his traveling companions to greet them. The birds were as drawn to St. Francis as he was to them. He asked them to stay and listen to the word of God, and they did. He preached to them, calling them his little sisters and urging them to praise their creator, God, who clothed them in feathers, gave them wings to fly, and provided for their every need. The birds were said to have careened their necks attentively and fluttered their wings joyfully, praising God as they were able to do according to their nature. It wasn't until he gave them his blessing, making the sign of the cross over them, that the flock took flight. The experience gave St. Francis pause. Why had he not preached to the birds and animals before? From then on, he made it part of his mission to teach all living beings about the goodness of God.

See also pages 29 and 179.
See also pages 196–97 for St. Francis's "Canticle of the Sun".

St. Gall

Memorial: October 16

Born in 550 in Ireland, St. Gall was educated by Sts. Columban and Comgall. He became a monk at Bangor, an Irish monastery that was a hub of mission work throughout Europe. He was one of St. Columban's twelve holy traveling companions with whom he evangelized and founded monasteries throughout France. In 612, St. Gall became ill and settled in Switzerland to recover. He lived as a hermit on the banks of the Steinach River, where he prayed and studied sacred Scripture. In his solitude, he communed deeply with nature, and birds were his constant companions. Furthering his association with birds, legend tells of an exorcism he once performed for a woman named Fridiburga, who was to be married to Sigebert II, the king of the Franks. More than one bishop had tried and failed to exorcise demons from her. St. Gall, however, succeeded. It is said the demons flew out of Fridiburga's mouth in the form of a flock of blackbirds. St. Gall, who died in Arbon, France, in 646, is considered the patron of all birds, in particular the patron of poultry.

See also page 67.

St. Isidore the Farmer

Memorial: May 15

This patron saint of farmers may also be considered a patron saint of birds. One cold winter day, St. Isidore walked to a grain mill with his coworkers, carrying a sack of corn on his shoulder. Spying some birds on a barren branch looking hungry and forlorn for lack of food, he took his sack and dumped half of its contents on the ground. Although the birds were delighted, his coworkers mocked his foolishness. Yet when St. Isidore and his companions arrived at the mill, his sack was full and miraculously yielded double the amount of grain as could be expected.

See also pages 31, 79, 152, and 165.
See also page 197 for a Prayer Invoking St. Isidore the Farmer.
See also page 218 for the Blessing of a Well.

St. Milburga
Memorial: February 23

A seventh-century daughter of English nobility, St. Milburga became a Benedictine nun as well as the founder and abbess of a monastery in Shropshire.
In addition to having brought a dead child back to life through her prayers,
it is said she exercised a mysterious power over birds. Stories are told of birds
taking flight from the farmers' fields at the sound of her simple request that
they cease damaging the crops. She is the patroness of both wild birds and pet
birds, as well as a protectress against damage to crops by birds.

St. Tryphon of Lampsacus
Memorial: February 1

Born around 222 in Phrygia, in modern-day Turkey, St. Tryphon was raised in
a Christian family. As a humble gooseherd, he was kind and devout. His prayers
were said to have healed both animals and humans. He also exorcised a demon
from the daughter of an emperor. His gifts of oration and teaching brought
about many conversions, which led to his martyrdom around 251. He is sometimes depicted in art in the company of a goose or with a falcon on his arm.

In the mid-1500s in Russia, a man named after St. Tryphon served as
Ivan the Terrible's hunting assistant. During one hunting excursion, Ivan's best
hunting falcon was lost. Poor Tryphon was blamed for the loss and was threatened with being beheaded if the bird wasn't found. After three days of searching in vain, Tryphon prayed to his namesake, asking for his help in locating
the falcon. Later that night in a dream, St. Tryphon appeared to assure him
of a favorable outcome. The next morning, Tryphon looked up and saw the
falcon in a pine tree. He returned the bird to Ivan, who, upon hearing about
the vision (and in a much better mood), ordered that a church dedicated to St.
Tryphon be built on the spot where Tryphon received the vision.

See also pages 12 and 108–09.

For the Protection of Blackbirds

St. Kevin of Glendalough
Memorial: July 3

As the story goes, one day, on the first day of Lent, St. Kevin stretched his arms out in prayer and lo, a blackbird came and laid an egg in the palm of his upturned hand. Not wishing to harm the egg and the creature within, he remained in that position for the duration of Lent—forty days—staying alive because the blackbird fed him wild berries and nuts. Once the baby bird was hatched and had flown from the nest of his palm, St. Kevin returned to the monastery.

He died at the age of 120, in 618. Although no one knows the precise location where St. Kevin is buried, it is said that the blackbirds do, and they flock to his unmarked grave at dusk to pay him homage.

While this story favors the blackbird, it is well known how destructive a flock of blackbirds can be to a farmer's crops. St. Kevin's friendship with blackbirds makes him the ideal saint to invoke when you need these winged pests to take flight!

See also pages 33–34, 65, and 141–42.

For the Protection of Geese

St. Achahildis of Wendelstein
Memorial: October 29

Of noble birth and the mother of quintuplets, St. Achahildis and her husband eventually took vows of celibacy, choosing to live in the world as charitable quasi-religious. In the tenth century, they founded a parish church in Wendelstein, Germany. According to legend, when St. Achahildis discovered that a poor servant had stolen and killed some geese for food, she not only forgave the servant but also brought the geese back to life—including one that had already been cooked, using just the leg bone to perform the miracle. St. Achahildis died around 970 of natural causes and is often represented in art with three geese or a goose leg.

St. Ambrose of Milan
Memorial: December 7

St. Ambrose's birth into the well-to-do family of the Roman prefect of Gaul, in Trier, Germany, privileged him with a first-hand understanding of the Roman culture that supported his masterful defense of the Christian faith. At one point, he argued to the Romans that it was the noisy outcry of geese, known for their watchman-like nature, that alerted the Roman emperor's soldiers that the Gauls were poised to infiltrate the walls of Rome and take the city, not their so-called god Jupiter. "Where then," he famously chastised, "was Jupiter? Or did he speak in goose?"

St. Ambrose, who in the fourth century served as the bishop in Milan, Italy, and who was instrumental in the conversion of St. Augustine, died of natural causes on Easter morning in 397 as the sun was rising over Milan.

See also page 69.

St. Kevin of Glendalough
Feast Day: July 3

When the king of Glendalough's beloved but aged pet goose began to show signs that he was failing and was no longer able to fly, the king summoned St. Kevin, whom he knew to be a holy man capable of working miracles. When St. Kevin arrived at the castle, the king beseeched him to make his goose young again. St. Kevin, who at the time was in search of land upon which to build a monastery in Glendalough, asked for whatever plot of land the goose would fly over in return for his intercession. The king agreed to St. Kevin's terms. Upon being held in St. Kevin's hands, the goose immediately completed a sweeping flight over an expansive valley that the king, true to his word, donated for the founding of the monastery.

See also pages 33–34, 64, and 141–42.

St. Martin of Tours
Feast Day: November 12

St. Martin was born in Pannonia, in modern-day Hungary, in 316. His father, an officer of the Roman army, dedicated the child to the god of war, Mars. When his father was reassigned to an area of Italy where Christianity was in bloom, St. Martin, a boy of fifteen, became a catechumen, much to his father's displeasure. In retaliation, his father had him drafted into the military. It was during a night patrol that a poor, semi-naked man appeared before him. St. Martin offered the man half of his military cloak; the next night in a dream, the same man revealed that he was Jesus. When St. Martin was discharged from the army in 354, his devotion and advancement in the faith was so rapid, in 371, the people of Tours elected him their bishop by acclamation. Wanting to avoid having to assume the position, preferring instead to continue evangelizing throughout the countryside, St. Martin hid amid a flock of geese, whose loud honking revealed his presence to the people, thereby leading to his inevitable rise as bishop of Tours.

St. Martin's feast day is said to overlap the migration of wild geese. The goose is the traditional fare of St. Martin's Day, a celebration held in advance of the Advent fast which, in the Middle Ages, began on November 12. In England, tradition dictates that if you have roast goose for Martinmas, you must ask St. Martin to dine with you (meaning, you must share your goose with someone who has none, just as St. Martin shared his cloak) or you will be without a goose the following year!

See also pages 48–49 and 120.

For the Protection of Chickens and Poultry

St. Bridget of Kildare
Memorial: February 1
St. Patrick, who was the compatriot and spiritual mentor of St. Bridget, attested that wild ducks, whether swimming in the water or flying in the air, obeyed the call of St. Bridget. They came to her and let her stroke and embrace them. She blessed them before releasing them to the air.

See also pages 32–33 and 90.

St. Gall
Memorial: October 16
Along with an eagle and a lamb, the cock, as a symbol of light and resurrection, is one of the more well-known emblems of Christ. Etymologically, St. Gall's name is connected to the Latin word *gallus*, meaning "cock," which may substantially form the basis for his patronage of poultry.

See also page 62.

St. Pharaildis of Ghent
Memorial: January 4
The daughter of a Belgian duke and his wife (St.) Amalberga, St. Pharaildis grew up surrounded by a constellation of saintly persons, including sisters, aunts, and a brother, all of whom were later canonized, not the least of whom was the aunt who raised her, St. Gertrude of Nivelles. She was married against her wishes, but remained a virgin. For thirty years she rose each day at the crow of the rooster so that she could hurry to the nearby monastery and pray the hours of prime, matins, and lauds. She is said to have walked on water, prayed geese away from the cornfields, brought a goose back from the dead, and struck the ground to bring forth a wellspring for the benefit of the farmers' harvest and for sick children who were cured by the water. She is also known for holy works and miracles, including turning the loaves of bread of a miserly woman into stones. She died around 740 of natural causes at the age of ninety.

Patrons of Bees and Hives

A holy trifecta of honey-tongued saints consists of St. Ambrose of Milan, St. Bernard of Clairvaux, and St. John Chrysostom, whose eloquence and oratory skills gained them great esteem. Collectively, they're known as the Doctores Melliflui, which roughly translates to "scholars sweet as honey." While the only formally designated patron saints of bees are Sts. Ambrose, Bernard of Clairvaux, and Modomnoc, there are other saints who merit an honorable mention.

For the Protection of Bees and Hives

St. Ambrose of Milan
Memorial: December 7

Born in 340 in Trier, in modern-day Germany, where his father was the prefect, legend states that while lying in his cradle, a swarm of bees lit upon the infant's lips, leaving drops of honey in and around his mouth. In those days, honey was likened to a mythical food of the gods, ambrosia, and so this event was interpreted as a sign that St. Ambrose had been gifted with eloquence. St. Ambrose did not disappoint. He was educated in Rome, where he studied law, literature, and rhetoric. He was made the governor of Liguria and Emilia in 372, and while not yet a baptized Christian, he was so effective in speech and generous in charity that the people clamored for him to become the bishop of Milan. Despite his reluctance to assume the position, in 374 in short order he was baptized, ordained, and consecrated the bishop of Milan. He was considered an "angel of God." He was St. Monica's holy mentor. He also baptized her once-wayward son, St. Augustine. It is said that he wrote the great Catholic hymn *Te Deum* in honor of Augustine's conversion to the Catholic faith. A doctor of the church, St. Ambrose died in 397.

See also page 65.

St. Benedict of Nursia

Memorial: July 11

Born in 480 in Nursia (Umbria), Italy, into a noble Roman family that included his pious twin sister, St. Scholastica, St. Benedict was expected to pursue a prestigious career in Roman government. After some years of study, Benedict became disillusioned by the emptiness of the world. He quit his studies and left Rome around 500. He settled first in a remote, mountainous town near Subiaco, then retreated into a nearby cave where he lived as a hermit for three years. His reputation for holiness spread, and he was eventually coaxed into becoming the abbot of a nearby monastery (where some dissolute monks tried to poison him). St. Benedict continued to write and refine his Rule for monks, which could also be adhered to by lay Christians. He founded many monasteries and schools, which gave rise to his title as the "Father of Western Monasticism." He died of a fever in Monte Cassino in 547.

St. Benedict's consideration as an ad-hoc patron saint of beekeepers and bees may stem from the fact that Benedictine monasteries were known for keeping hives for the production of candles made of beeswax, as well as honey for food and for the production of mead. In some areas of France, it is customary to have a St. Benedict medal attached to the hives.

See also pages 77–78.

St. Bernard of Clairvaux

Memorial: August 20

The third of seven children, St. Bernard was born in France in 1090 to a family that observed intense devotion to the Blessed Mother. Following his studies, he entered the Cistercian community in 1112, and founded a new Cistercian monastery at Clairvaux, where he served as abbot, and attracted many postulants. He left the cloistered life to use his gifts of preaching, teaching, and mediation so that he could help restore order and unity in both church and political arenas, and to refute heretical teachings, which gave rise to him being referred to as the Hammer of Heretics. Yet he was also by nature a poet, and the sweetness of his preaching engendered another moniker, the Honey-Sweet Doctor. Unsurprisingly, he is often represented in art and iconography with a beehive. He died in 1153 at Clairvaux Abbey in northeastern France.

St. John Chrysostom
Memorial: September 13

A doctor of the church who was renowned for the sweetness of his preaching, St. John Chrysostom was born in 357 in Antioch, Syria. As a young adult, he pursued a career in law. However, after having been baptized at the age of twenty-three, he forsook a career in law for a life of service to the Lord. He entered a monastery and was ordained in 386. The popularity of his preaching led to a post as the Patriarchate and, later, bishop of Constantinople. In his 12th Homily, he famously wrote, "The bee is more honored than other animals, not because she labors, but because she labors for others."

He devoted himself to rooting out corruption both within as well as outside of the clergy. His efforts often incurred the wrath of the empress, who eventually banished him from Constantinople. He spent his remaining years in exile, though he continued to offer eloquent homilies, writings, and commentaries in service to his flock and to his beloved church. St. John Chrysostom, the Golden Mouth, died in Pontus in 407.

St. Modomnoc
Memorial: February 13

Born in the sixth century into a royal Irish clan, St. Modomnoc relocated to Wales to further his religious education. While a novice there, he became a beekeeper who studied, conversed with, and cared for the bees. He introduced bees to his native land because at the time of his departure for Ireland, his beloved bees swarmed his boat and refused to let him leave without them. He became the bishop of Ossory, Ireland, and died in 550 of natural causes.

St. Valentine of Rome
Memorial: February 14

Persecuted by the Roman emperor Claudius II for officiating the marriages of Christian couples and for aiding imprisoned Christians, the Roman priest St. Valentine was beheaded in 269. One legend asserts that while he was imprisoned, St. Valentine healed the jailer's blind daughter. Before his execution, he left a note of encouragement and affection for the girl, signing it simply, "Your Valentine." Best known as the patron saint of lovers, his association with bees is likely a tribute to the sweetness of love.

———————

Part II

Patron Saints of Farm-Related People and Occupations

Sometimes the association of a saint with a given occupation is merely due to his or her patronage of the corresponding animal. In these cases, a simple cross reference is made.

Rumination

I confess to loving a room with a view, all the better if it doesn't have actual walls. A canopy of sky for a ceiling, white pines and pin oaks on every side, and a rolling carpet of pasture grass under my feet form my daily workspace. This farm isn't just where I work and play; it has also become a breezy outdoor abbey of sorts where, over time, I have learned to work and pray. But it wasn't always so.

As the novelty of being a second-career farmer faded, barn chores turned into darn chores. Caring for our land and livestock became a grinding, full-time job. The Fourth Commandment became my personal favorite. Sitting in a pew instead of behind the wheel of a tractor gave me a chance to focus on prayer and the presence of God. Farming and homesteading were like that for some time, until I found the rhythm, until I found the rhyme. Let me explain.

St. Benedict, the industrious, sixth-century abbot and a patron saint of farmers and field hands, had a motto that girded the monastic life he lived and pioneered. *Ora et labora.* Pray and work. To know it is one thing. To live it is another. Learning to integrate the rhythm of labor and prayer into my daily life has gradually transformed my grind into glory; so much so that the welcome sign at the bottom of our hill announces the motto of Flying Chestnut Farm: *Soli Deo Gloria.* Glory to God alone.

Now when I throw hay for the horses, I thank God for what will be sweet nourishment in their mouths and warmth in their bellies. I measure out grain and pray for the harvesters. I draw water and carry buckets and think of Photina, the woman at the well. The lambs gather, drink their fill, and clamor for my attention. I sigh and flip an empty bucket upside down and sit with them for a spell. I'm not slacking, I remind myself. I'm making room for bliss.

I think of the many shepherd-saints who found both refuge and bliss in the tending of their flocks. Though they suffered deep poverty or extreme childhood cruelties, by God's grace their faith and devotion only deepened. St. Solange, a poor virgin shepherdess and martyr, dedicated herself to God and was often seen praying in the fields, accompanied by a shining star over her head. Another shepherdess, St. Germaine Cousin, was content to sleep on a pallet in the barn near the animals rather than in a house where there was no love. She stole off to attend daily Mass, leaving her sheep in the care of her guardian angel, and never did one go missing.

What these and other patron saints have taught me is that my barn chores are only darn chores when I'm a farmer who has only roots and no wings with which to fly to heaven. Following their lead, my days have become a rolling liturgy of the hours. There are prayers at sunrise as I lean into the pasture gate and step into my panoramic abbey. There are Angelus bells that ring in my soul and summon me to prayer at noon. And there is the tabernacle of twilight, when the day is done and I can do no more but gaze into a sapphire sky with gratitude, wonder, and awe.

Ora et labora. This is the rhythm. This is the rhyme.

I no longer have to wait for Sunday to find rest and relief. I humbly suggest, neither do you. There are inexhaustible reserves to be found when we remain in communion with these humble, hardworking patron saints who encourage us and intercede on our behalf. As we farm and homestead on the land we love, let us hold dear the image of St. Solange, who knelt in dirt and bathed in light.

Ora et labora!

For the Protection of Farmers, Farmworkers, and Field Hands

St. Andrew the Apostle
Memorial: November 30

Born at Bethsaida, Galilee, St. Andrew was among the first disciples called by Jesus. A fisherman by trade, he abandoned his livelihood to follow Christ. After the crucifixion of Jesus, St. Andrew preached the gospel throughout Asia Minor and Greece. He was martyred in 60 on an X-shaped cross, where he heroically preached for two days before dying. Legend holds that in the fourth century, the saint's relics were brought from Patras, Greece, to Kinrymont in Fife, Scotland, by St. Regulus of Scotland. The church at Kinrymont became the cathedral of St. Andrew and served as a major destination for medieval pilgrimages. St. Andrew has been honored in Scotland for over a thousand years, with feasts dating back to 1000. It wasn't until 1320, however, that he became the country's official patron saint. His early patronage of Scotland, a country known for its extensive sheep, beef cattle, and pig farms, as well as its legendary cereal crops and potato farms, led farmers to look to St. Andrew for divine help in all their agricultural needs.

See also page 86.

St. Benedict of Nursia
Memorial: July 11

Born in 480 in Nursia, Italy, to a noble Roman family that included his pious twin sister, St. Scholastica, St. Benedict was expected to pursue a prestigious career in Roman government. Having become disillusioned by the emptiness of the world, he quit his studies and left Rome around the year 500. He traveled with his servant to a community of like-minded men in Enfide, a remote village located on a mountain crest about forty miles outside of Rome. There, he miraculously restored to pristine condition an earthenware wheat sifter (*capisterium*) which his servant had accidentally broken. The miracle brought much unwanted attention to the young Benedict. He reacted by retreating even more deeply into isolation. He fled to a ten-foot mountaintop cave that overlooked a pristine lake near Subiaco, where he lived for the next three years.

It's likely that the *capisterium* miracle contributed to his association with farmers, particularly those growing wheat, as did the legend of how his prayers during a time of famine miraculously resulted in two hundred bushels of flour being delivered to a large community of friars who were down to their last five loaves of bread.

It is also said that during his three years of solitude, he became known to the local shepherds who tended flocks on the lower hills as their Saint of the Mountain. They brought him offerings of milk and cheese and asked for his blessing and prayers in return. His intercession was so effective, he was beseeched by a nearby company of monks to become their abbot. He accepted the position, and it was during this period that he wrote the *Rule of St. Benedict,* which even today governs Benedictine monasteries throughout the world. Considered the Father of Western Monasticism, he died in 547 of a fever at the Abbey of Monte Cassino, in Italy.

See also page 70.

St. Bernard of Vienne
Memorial: January 22

Born in Lyons, France, to wealthy landowners, St. Bernard of Vienne married and became a military officer in the ranks of Charlemagne. He returned home after seven years, buried his parents, and divested his family's vast farmlands by donating one-third to the church, one-third to the poor, and one-third to his children. Thereafter, he purchased and then entered a monastery in Ambronay. His piety and learning set him apart as an abbot, then as the arch-bishop of Vienne from 810 until his death in 842. He is honored in the Dauphiny region as the patron saint of farmworkers, presumably a nod to the dispensation of his inheritance to the poor people who were able to earn a living on that land.

St. Botulph
Memorial: June 17

Born in 610 in Saxon (modern England) to devout Christian parents of noble rank, as a young man St. Botulph relocated to Gaul (northeastern France) to escape political upheaval and continue his studies. He became a Benedictine monk, after which he was recalled to the British Isles to establish another monastery. For his new monastery, he chose a barren site in a wilderness believed to be haunted by demons. A growing community of devout men joined him and, together, persisted in labors that turned marshland and heavy scrub into fertile farming and grazing acreage. Meanwhile, their prayerfulness and bold faith had the effect of eradicating the citizen's fears of demons. He was said to be a congenial man who was beloved by all. He died around 700.

St. Isidore the Farmer
Memorial: May 15

Considered by many to be the primary patron saint of farming, St. Isidore is the go-to intercessor for all people, places, and concerns of an agricultural nature.

See also pages 31, 62, 152, and 165.
See also page 197 for a Prayer Invoking St. Isidore the Farmer.
See also page 218 for the Blessing of a Well.

St. Leonard of Noblac
Memorial: November 6

A portion of the vast, forested land in Noblat, located in the Limousin region of France, was granted to St. Leonard by royal decree for the purpose of building a monastery. This land allowed former prisoners to get a fresh start as farmers who would be able to make a decent living. As a hermit, St. Leonard himself lived off the land and quenched his thirst with spring water. Following his death in 559 of natural causes, more than four thousand favors are said to have been granted in one Bavarian town as a result of his powerful intercessions.

See also pages 47–48.

St. Lucy of Syracuse
Memorial: December 13

St. Lucy, a late first-century virgin martyr from Syracuse, Italy, avoided being forced into an arranged marriage by consecrating herself to Christ. Her jilted fiancé denounced her as a Christian to the governor of Sicily. Her sentence was forced prostitution, but when the prison guards came for her, God rendered her immovable. Even a team of oxen hitched to her body could not move her from the cell. She was tortured, blinded (she is a patroness of the blind), and killed on the spot.

Originating from the bizarre torture she endured, St. Lucy is most often depicted with her eyeballs in a dish. However, her representation as a woman hitched to a yoke of straining oxen may account for the association with farm-workers. Adding to the cause is the report that she, in her youth, along with her noble mother, who long suffered from a hemorrhagic illness, donated land to the local peasants in gratitude for her mother's miraculous healing through St. Agnes's intercession. St. Lucy died in 304.

See also page 181.

St. Nicholas of Myra
Memorial: December 6

The son of pious aged parents, St. Nicholas, who came to be known as Santa Claus, was ordained a priest at an early age and thereafter dedicated himself to caring for the poor. His uncle, the archbishop of Myra (in Asia Minor), put him in charge of a monastery, but after the death of his uncle, St. Nicholas was consecrated the new archbishop of Myra. Soon after his appointment, the entire province suffered a terrible famine. When Nicholas learned that three ships laden with wheat had arrived at the port, he went to the shore to beg the sailors to give something of their store to alleviate the hunger of his people. The sailors refused on the grounds that the wheat, which they were transporting to the emperor, had already been measured at Alexandria. St. Nicholas promised the sailors that their cargo would not show any diminishment when they delivered it to the emperor, and his word proved true. St. Nicholas distributed among the people the wheat he had been given, some of which was set aside for sowing. The wheat lasted a miraculously long time, feeding the local citizens for two years. St. Nicholas died in Myra in 342.

See also pages 88–89, 110–11, 114, 121, 125, 133–34, and 182.

St. Notburga of Eben
Memorial: September 14

The patroness of female agricultural workers, St. Notburga was born in 1265 to a family of milliners who lived in the Tyrolian region of Bavaria, Austria. In her late teens she became a kitchen maid to a count and countess who resided in *Schloss* ("Castle") Rattenberg. At first, the count and countess did not object to her great piety as evidenced in her practice of supplying bread and wine to the poor in their community. But the nobles underwent a change of heart and forbade St. Notburga to care for the poor. Eventually, they fired her. St. Notburga fled to St. Rupert's Chapel, which was in Eben on the other side of the river from the castle. She negotiated with a local farmer to work as a servant in his fields, provided they allow her to attend church the evening before Sundays and festivals. Once, while working in the fields, her employer demanded that all field hands work overtime to complete the harvest. St. Notburga alone refused, laying down her sickle and reminding him of the contract they had struck. The farmer persisted, and in response St. Notburga prayed to God to provide a sign of his allegiance with the overworked farmhands. When Notburga raised her sickle, saying, "Let my sickle be judge between me and you!" it miraculously floated in the air. She returned to Rattenberg following the death of the countess, and, with the count's blessing, resumed her charitable works and the distribution of bread and wine to the poor. She died in 1313 of natural causes and is buried in Eben. She is represented with an ear of corn, or flowers, and a sickle in her hand; alternately, with a sickle suspended in the air.

St. Phocas the Gardener
Memorial: July 3 (alternately, also July 23 and September 22)

A humble farmer, innkeeper, and gardener, St. Phocas was a Christian martyr who was beheaded in 303 in Sinope, Pontus (modern-day Turkey). He was known for using his surplus crops to feed the poor, which he did in the name of Christ. The local authorities, having heard there was a Christian living nearby, sent two Roman soldiers to execute him. It was evening when the soldiers came upon a peasant laboring in his fields. The peasant, none other than St. Phocas, bade them to stay with him given the lateness of the hour, and then showered them with hospitality. Upon learning of their intentions, St. Phocas told the soldiers that he was well acquainted with the man they sought and promised to lead them to him in the morning. St. Phocas spent the night digging his own grave and preparing his soul to meet God. In the morning, he admitted to the soldiers that he was the Christian they sought to execute. They overcame their initial reluctance to harm him in light of his hospitality, killing him by cutting off his head.

See also pages 17–18 and 107.

St. Procopius
Memorial: July 14

An Eastern Rite priest, monk, and hermit who lived in what is now modern-day Hungary during the eleventh century, St. Procopius's widespread holiness and miracles of healing drew the attention of the duke of Oldrich, in Bohemia, who assisted him in founding an Eastern Rite monastery in Prague. Procopius served as abbot of that monastery for twenty years, until his death. Legend states that the saint once hitched the devil to a plow and forced him to plow a deep furrow along a riverbank. He is most often represented as a man tilling with a devil pulling the plow.

St. Walburga
Memorial: February 25

Born in the early eighth century, St. Walburga was the daughter of Richard, the king of Wessex, and studied at a monastery in Dorset, England, where she later became a nun. In the mid-700s, she undertook a mission to what is now Germany, evangelizing and miraculously healing pagans throughout the country. Following her death in 779, her relics were placed on a rock, which is said to exude oil with miraculous healing properties, reminiscent of the powerful healings she performed during her lifetime. The oil is said to cure plague, rabies, coughs, and fit-inducing afflictions.

The evening before the first of May, which commemorates the translation of the saint's relics to Eichstätt in 870, is known as *Walpurgisnacht*, which coincides with a pagan festival marking the beginning of summer. Over time, the lines between the festivals blurred, and St. Walburga became associated with the protection of crops provided by Mother Earth and celebrated on May Day, a pagan holiday. Hence, her icons depict her as an abbess holding three ears of corn.

However, an obscure legend also tells of St. Walburga's late-night, prayer-inspired visit to the home of a nearly destitute land baron whose farmland had become desolate. He was a huntsman, and though his dogs encircled the nun and barked menacingly at her, none of them harmed her. The baron was so astonished, he became fearful, and begged her to leave. St. Walburga assured him that if he would but believe with his whole heart that God is the true physician who has power over life and death, health and consolation would return to his house. At these words, the believing baron threw open a door that looked out upon his meadows, and before his very eyes they began to bloom and provide ample crops.

See also page 174.

St. Walstan of Bawburgh
Memorial: May 30

Born in Bawburgh, England, in 975, St. Walstan felt a deep devotion to God from a very young age. At the age of twelve, he forsook his father's princely home and noble rank, choosing instead to work as an itinerant farmhand on the outskirts of Taverham, near Norwich. He showed great deference to the poor, often giving away whatever food he possessed, as well as his shoes, though he was left barefoot. God honored his humility by empowering his prayers to bring about many miraculous cures of people and animals.

One of his employers had such a fondness for the good-hearted saint that he offered to make him an heir. The humble St. Walstan declined the offer and continued to work his employer's land for the next thirty years. Finally, at the providential urging of an angel of God, he accepted gifts of two white calves and a small wagon. In May of 1066, at the start of haymaking, St. Walston was visited by an angel who foretold his impending death, which would take place in three days. On the last of those three days, having summoned a priest to the field where he was working to provide Holy Communion, St. Walstan instructed that his body should be laid on the wagon he had been given and driven by the two white calves to whatever place of rest they might choose. A miraculous spring appeared so that the priest could wash his hands in preparation for the consecration. Upon receiving communion, St. Walstan prayed to God that every sick farm laborer and animal should obtain healing of their infirmities, provided they ask for the healings with humility and devotion. At that, St. Walstan expired, and a white dove was seen flying upward. The calves pulling the wagon on which his body was loaded passed dry-shod through the river and into the church at Bawburgh. They entered through an opening in a wall made by an angel, which promptly closed up behind them. Today, water from miraculous springs attributed to St. Walstan is still sought by pilgrims to heal themselves and their beloved farm animals.

For the Protection of Bird Breeders and Dealers

St. John the Baptist
Memorial: June 24

St. John is said to have been imprisoned up until the time of his martyrdom in a cell that had the appearance of a cage. For that reason, he became associated with birds who are kept in cages for breeding or other commercial purposes. His patronage of bird breeders and dealers may also be connected to his pivotal role in the baptism of Jesus, upon whom the Holy Spirt descended in the form of a dove.

See also pages 56–57 and 186.

For the Protection of Beekeepers

In addition to those saints who are patrons of bees, St. Ambrose of Milan (see pages 65 and 69), St. Bernard of Clairvaux (see pages 70–71), and St. Valentine of Rome (see page 72) also serve as patron saints of beekeepers.

For the Protection of Butchers

St. Adrian of Nicomedia
Memorial: September 8

An officer in the bodyguard of Roman Emperor Galerius at the turn of the fourth century, St. Adrian witnessed, in his official capacity, the trial and torture of twenty-two Christians. Deeply impressed by their courage and immovable faith, he declared himself a Christian, and was thrown into prison. He died at the hands of executioners who butchered him, hewing his legs, thighs, arms, and hands. His body and the bodies of his fellow prisoners were thrown into a raging fire.

However, such a fierce rainstorm descended over the conflagration, the bodies were not consumed by the fire. The storm gave fellow Christians an opportunity to carry away the bodies and limbs for safekeeping and veneration. St. Adrian's relics were translated to Constantinople, then to Rome, and then to Flanders, where many miracles occurred owing to his powerful intercession.

St. Andrew the Apostle
Memorial: November 30
The iconic images of St. Andrew and a wild boar acquired a special significance in 1502 when a giant boar that reportedly had killed both men and cattle was slain near the town of St. Andrews. Its sixteen-inch tusks were then attached to the high altar of the cathedral. It's likely that this connection forms the basis for St. Andrew's popularity with local butchers, whose specialties include the making of sausage from wild boar.

See also page 77.

St. Anthony the Abbot
Memorial: January 17
It is believed that St. Anthony the Abbot kept close company with animals for the twenty years he lived as a hermit, giving rise to his status as a patron of domestic animals and farm stock, which, of course, includes swine. It's likely this association with swine prompted the patronage of butchers—a curious connection given that St. Anthony was a strict vegetarian.

See also pages 28–29, 57–58, and 96.

St. Bartholomew the Apostle
Memorial: August 24
St. Bartholomew (also known as Nathanael) was born in Galilee. He was a close companion of St. Philip, who introduced him to Jesus. St. Bartholomew was one of the twelve apostles. Following the resurrection of Christ, he is said to have preached in Asia Minor, Ethiopia, India, and Armenia, where, according to legend, he converted Polymius, the king of Armenia. The king's brother,

fearing a Roman backlash, ordered the execution of St. Bartholomew who was flayed, crucified upside down, and left to die. Michelangelo's *The Last Judgment* depicts the saint holding his own skin, which gave rise to his cult status as the patron saint of butchers and tanners.

St. John the Apostle
Memorial: December 27

St. John the Apostle, son of Zebedee and Salome, became a disciple of St. John the Baptist. Known as "the beloved disciple," St. John was the only apostle who remained at the foot of the cross. It was to St. John that Jesus entrusted the care of Mary, his mother.

St. John was once imprisoned with St. Peter for sharing the gospel. He suffered further persecution when the Roman emperor Domitian had him thrown into a cauldron of boiling oil, from which St. John emerged unscathed. In frustration, the emperor banished him to the island of Patmos, in Greece. It was here that St. John wrote the fourth Gospel, three epistles, and the book of Revelation. He was eventually released from exile, and died in Ephesus, Turkey, circa 101. Butchers may have likened St. John's immersion in a vat of boiling oil to the way butchered meat was commonly prepared, and so adopted St. John as their patron saint.

See also pages 119, 147, and 186.

St. Lawrence
Memorial: August 10

An archdeacon of Rome in the mid-third century, St. Lawrence was known as the "keeper of the treasures of the church" at a time when Christians were undergoing intense persecutions by the Roman emperor Valerian. A vicious round of executions left St. Lawrence as the highest-ranking representative of the church in Rome. Warned of his impending arrest, he made haste to distribute the material wealth of the church before the Romans could seize it. On August 10, he was arraigned before Valerian and was commanded to bring with him the treasures of the church to hand over to the Roman authorities. Having dispersed the church's wealth, he instead brought with him Rome's poor, crippled, and sick citizens, declaring them the true treasures of the church. In a fury, Valerian ordered St. Lawrence to be grilled over gridirons, which led to his martyrdom in 258. This accounts for his patronage of cooks and those who work in or supply kitchens—such as butchers. Tradition states that the ashes of his body were scattered by the wind and appear around the world on his feast day.

See also pages 119–120 and 181.

St. Luke the Evangelist
Memorial: October 18
Believed to be the author of the Gospel that bears his name, as well as of the Acts of the Apostles, St. Luke was born in Antioch (Syria) to a wealthy Greek family, received training as a physician, and was said to have traveled as a ship's doctor. He accompanied St. Paul on his second missionary journey and likely cared for the ailing apostle to the Gentiles up to and during his last days of imprisonment in Rome. According to tradition, St. Luke wrote his Gospel in Greece, where he died at the age of eighty-four around 74.

In art, Luke is represented by a winged ox (a castrated male bull of the bovine [cattle] species) which likely accounts for his patronage of butchers. In the Old Testament, the prophet Ezekiel dreamed of four winged creatures supporting the throne of God, one of which was a winged ox. This is especially appropriate because in the Gospel of St. Luke, the priestly and sacrificial work of Jesus is emphasized. The ox represents the sacrificial aspect of Jesus' ministry (oxen were commonly sacrificed in Old Testament times), and the wings remind us that the gospel of Jesus Christ is to travel throughout the world.

St. Nicholas of Myra
Memorial: December 6
Legends abound of the good and charitable deeds performed by St. Nicholas of Myra. Many of St. Nicholas's actions were in the role as a heroic protector of children. One such occasion, according to a French tradition, was when three small children wandered off during their playtime and became lost. They were lured and captured by an evil butcher who cut them to pieces and put their remains in a salting tub, or brine barrel, to cure. The butcher was planning to

pass them off as ham. St. Nicholas suddenly appeared and demanded that the butcher open his salting tub. The butcher complied. St. Nicholas, placing his hand in the tub, appealed to God to restore the children to life and to their families. The children were miraculously resurrected. As the story goes, the repentant butcher became St. Nicholas's lifelong servant. Thus it is no wonder that the image of St. Nicholas with children in a tub at his feet is the most prominent image of the saint throughout Western Europe.

See also pages 80–81, 110–11, 114, 121, 125, 133–34, and 182.

St. Peter the Apostle
Memorial: June 29

Born in Bethsaida in Galilee as "Simon" son of Jonah, a fisherman by family trade and the brother of St. Andrew the apostle, who led him to Christ, Simon was given the name *Peter* (meaning "rock") by Jesus to symbolize the foundation of the church that St. Peter would provide as its first pope. Though once having denied knowing Christ three times, he became a fearless evangelist and wonder-worker, and eventually a martyr who was crucified upside down in Rome by the Roman emperor Nero in 67. His loose association with butchers likely stems from the story told in the three synoptic Gospels about the companion of Jesus who, amid the drama of Christ's arrest, cut off the ear of a servant of the High Priest. The Gospel of John names St. Peter as the swordsman who, in effect, butchered the victim's ear.

See also page 111.

For the Protection of Dairy Workers

St. Bridget of Kildare
Memorial: February 1

The patroness of Ireland, St. Bridget exercised great care for the local poor, often giving away milk and butter. Her association as the patron saint of dairy workers naturally arises from her activities as a dairy maid on the family farm.

See also pages 32–33 and 67.

For the Protection of Cowherds

St. Gummarus
Memorial: October 11

An eighth-century nobleman of Brabant, in the province of Antwerp (Belgium), St. Gummarus was indoctrinated into the court of King Pepin the Short. He was known to be God-fearing and exceedingly kind, and especially careful not to let a cross or impure word form on his lips. The king was so pleased with his piousness that he gave him the hand of a high noblewoman—who turned out to be a veritable shrew with no real love for the virtuous St. Gummarus. The king enlisted St. Gummarus to fight wars in Lombardy and Saxony, and the care of his lands was left to his wicked wife, who treated the servants and farmhands with great disdain and cruelty; some were dismissed, others were forced to draw the plows with their own hands, or they were yoked, instead of oxen, to the carts. When the war ended and Gummarus returned home, he learned of his wife's cruel conduct, severely reprimanded her, and restored the dignity and livelihoods of the cowherds, servants, and other farmhands in his employ. When his attempts to convert his wife to Christianity failed, he later separated from her and became a hermit. Near the end of his life, he founded an abbey at Lier, Belgium, and died in 774 of natural causes.

For the Protection of Shepherds and Shepherdesses

St. Bernadette of Lourdes
Memorial: April 16 (alternately, February 18)

At fourteen years old and as a simple, poor shepherdess from a destitute family, St. Bernadette was the only girl in her village who had yet to make her first communion. This was due to the opportunistic nature of her employer—her former wet nurse who insisted she spend her time caring for the sheep on her farm instead of attending religious (or any other) education. This absence of education gave rise to great skepticism when she professed to have had a vision of a beautiful woman in a grotto near Lourdes, France, in February of 1858.

That was the first of seventeen visions of the Blessed Virgin Mary experienced by St. Bernadette at the rock of Massabielle near Lourdes. During one of those visits, the Blessed Mother instructed Bernadette to dig the ground with her hands at the grotto, drink the water that trickled forth, and wash her face with the water. The following day, the trickle turned into a flowing spring that to this day produces upwards of 27,000 gallons of water per day, the source of the healing water that draws millions of pilgrims to Lourdes. In subsequent appearances, perhaps owing to St. Bernadette's humility and obedience, the Blessed Mother revealed herself to her as the Immaculate Conception.

In the years that followed, St. Bernadette became increasingly weary of attention from the public. At the age of twenty, she entered the novitiate of the order of the Sisters of Charity and Christian Instruction, where she tended to the sick. She herself suffered from severe asthma; during one particularly fierce attack, she requested water from the spring at Lourdes and was permanently cured by it. Her health declined in other ways, however, and she died in 1879 at the age of thirty-five. She was sealed in a casket and buried on the convent grounds. Upon exhumation in 1908, her body was found incorrupt, and now reposes in a glass reliquary in a convent chapel in central France.

St. Cuthman of Steyning
Memorial: February 8

An ancient stone set high above the heather on the moors near Cornwall, England, marks the spot where St. Cuthman is said to have kept watch over his father's sheep in the eighth century. From this vantage point, he would draw a circle with the tip of his staff and command his flock, in the name of Christ, to remain at rest until he returned from gathering food for his sustenance. The sheep never strayed. Before long, the locals began to take note of his extraordinary piety and unusual herding abilities. Following the death of his father, however, he and his sick, paralyzed mother were destitute. Unable to provide for her needs, he fashioned a wheelbarrow yoked by a rope to his shoulders, then proceeded to carry his mother along as he begged door-to-door for their provision. He pushed the barrow eastward, leaving the moors. He dreamed of one day building a church. When the ropes frayed and broke, he took it as a divine sign that they'd found the place where he and his mother were to settle down. He prayed, "O Almighty Father, who has brought my journey to an end, You know how poor I am, a labourer from my youth, and of myself I can do nothing unless You succor me." Then he built a hut for himself and his mother (no surprise that he is also the patron saint of bachelors) and set about measuring the ground for what would become the church he founded near Steyning in Sussex, not far from the River Adur. He was buried beside that river, at a place that came to be known as St. Cuthman's Port.

St. Dominic de Silos
Memorial: December 20

St. Dominic was a shepherd boy in Navarre, Spain, before becoming a Benedictine monk at Silos, in Castile, Spain. Time spent in the fields imparted a deep appreciation for solitude, thereby making him well suited for monastic life. In the eleventh century, the abbey over which he was appointed abbot was in a state of extreme degradation. Under his leadership, the abbey was restored to a condition of beauty and goodness such that it became one of the most famous in all of Spain. It is said that St. Dominic performed many miraculous works there, including the healing of the blind, deaf, and mute. He died in 1073 of natural causes.

Another St. Dominic—founder of the Dominican Order—was named by his mother after St. Dominic of Silos in gratitude for a safe and successful pregnancy, which she prayed for at his tomb in Silo, Spain.

St. Germaine Cousin
Memorial: June 15

Often depicted with a shepherd's crook or a sheep at her side, St. Germaine was born in 1579 near Toulouse in southern France. Her mother died shortly after her birth. Her father, a farmworker, sorely neglected her, a sorrow that was compounded by her sickly nature. Raised by an abusive stepmother, she was forced to sleep under the stairs or in the stable, and was regularly beaten for imagined misdeeds.

At the age of nine, she was assigned the care of the sheep, and she happily made the fields her sanctuary. She prayed the rosary on a handmade string of knots. Each day, she stole off to Mass, leaving her flock under the care of her guardian angel. Never did a sheep go missing or suffer harm in her absence. She catechized the local poor children in the field and shared what little food she had with them. She died on her straw pallet under the stairs at the age of twenty-two. More than four hundred documented miracles have been attributed to her intercession. She is also the patron saint of rural girls.

Bl. Panacea of Quarona
Memorial: March 27

Born in Quarona, Italy, in the mid-fourteenth century, Bl. Panacea suffered the early sudden death of her mother. She was raised by Margherita, a stepmother who had no love for religion of any kind. Panacea drew the ire of her stepmother for supposedly shirking her chores in favor of prayer, and she was subjected to frequent beatings. She was sent out into the fields to care for the sheep. One spring evening when Bl. Panacea was fifteen years old, she went to the hermitage of San Giovanni to pray. Her stepmother went out looking for her, and upon finding Bl. Panacea in prayer instead of in the pastures, she flew into such a fit of rage, she beat Bl. Panacea to death (other accounts say she murdered her with a spindle). Horrified by what she'd done, Margherita threw herself into a nearby ravine and perished. Bl. Panacea was buried next to her birth mother on May 1, and by the beginning of the fifteenth century, the cult of Panacea was already widespread, with two oratories dedicated to her at the place where she died. It remains a popular place of pilgrimage, particularly on the first Friday of May.

St. Paschal Baylon
Memorial: May 17

Born in the sixteenth century to poor and pious Spanish parents, St. Paschal tended his family's sheep from the age of seven until twenty-four. While working in the fields, he often carried books with him and would implore anyone whom he met to teach him to read. Once he had mastered the skill, he became a voracious reader of holy books, and his knowledge of and devotion to Christ increased accordingly. He developed a great love for the poor, often sharing his meager meals with them. Weary of the foolishness and lack of virtue demonstrated by his fellow shepherds, he eventually entered a community of barefoot, reformed Franciscans as a lay brother, where he tended the front door and cooked in the kitchen. His piety and advancement in the faith soon earned him the name of the Holy Shepherd. Besides being a patron of shepherds, he is also known as the Saint of the Eucharist. He died in 1592 in Spain of natural causes.

St. Raphael the Archangel
Memorial: September 29

One of God's archangels and one of only three angels named in the Bible, St. Raphael takes the lead role in the book of Tobit as the divine traveling companion and guardian of Tobiah. St. Raphael is also associated with the healing waters of the Sheep Pool, as referenced in John 5:1–9.

The Sheep Pool (the Pool of Bethesda) is near the Sheep Gate on the north end of the Temple Mount in Jerusalem. The Gate, mentioned by the Old Testament prophet Nehemiah, takes its name from having been the port of entry for sheep brought to the temple for sacrifice. The pool itself, which in Old Testament times was located outside the city to the north, would have been used to wash the sheep beforehand, and was also a water source used by the shepherds. At the time of Christ, a twin pool fed by the upper pool was located inside the Sheep Gate. It was a spring-fed pool which, owing to its gross association with the upper pool, was used only by the lowliest and poorest Jews to wash themselves before entering the temple. It naturally became a gathering place for invalids, who waited for its water to be stirred. Although the stirring of the Sheep Pool—which gave the water the temporary power to cure—could be attributed to the fact that it was spring fed, it was believed to occur by the hand of an angel. This angel came to be identified as Raphael.

St. Regina
Memorial: September 7
Born in Burgundy, France, in the third century to an aristocratic, pagan family, St. Regina was raised by her Christian nurse after her mother died during childbirth. She was banished from her home by her father in punishment for her conversion to Christianity. Thereafter, she worked in the fields as a poor, devout shepherdess until her beauty caught the eye of Olybrius, the Roman prefect of Gaul. When she refused to renounce her faith and marry him, she was imprisoned, repeatedly tortured on the rack, and ultimately beheaded in 286. It is said that over eight hundred pagans converted as a result of her Christian witness and martyrdom at the tender age of sixteen.

St. Simeon Stylites
Memorial: July 27
A shepherd boy in his youth, St. Simeon was born around 390 in Cilicia, near Syria. After hearing a sermon on the Beatitudes, he became a monk and entered a nearby monastery at the age of sixteen. However, his superiors eventually deemed him unsuitable for community life due to his self-inflicted penances. God led St. Simeon to a more austere life. In 423, he lived as a hermit perched on top of a six-foot column that he increased in height over decades of time; he prayed and preached from its summit for the remainder of his life. It is said the pillar was sixty feet high and three feet wide at the time of his death. He incited a movement of other pillar dwellers and died in 459 of natural causes. His name, Simeon Stylites, is derived from the Greek word *stylos*, which signifies a pillar.

St. Solange
Memorial: May 10

A virgin shepherdess who tended her father's sheep and dedicated herself to God, it is said that whenever St. Solange prayed in the fields near Bourges, France, she was accompanied by a shining star over her head. She is also said to have had a great love of animals as well as the power to heal them. Born in 863, her vow of chastity led her to be martyred at the age of seventeen by one of the sons of the count of Poitiers, who stabbed her with a knife for refusing his sexual advances. She is commonly portrayed in art as a shepherdess with a star over her head, and with a crucifix nearby.

See also page 166.

For the Protection of Swineherds

St. Anthony the Abbot
Memorial: January 17

St. Anthony's association with swineherds arises in part from the tale of a fierce battle he undertook with Satan, in the form of a ferocious pig, who repeatedly attacked while St. Anthony was on a year-long retreat. St. Anthony resisted Satan's assaults with such quiet fortitude and saintly grace, the possessed pig was transformed into a docile, devoted companion. Perhaps it is this very pig that gave rise to the term Tantony Pig—a Middle-Ages contraction of "St. Anthony's Pig," a somewhat derogatory name for someone who blindly follows others.

See also pages 28–29, 57–58, and 86.
See also page 220 for a Blessing of Lard.

For the Protection of Horsemen, Horsewomen, and Equestrians

St. Anne
Memorial: July 26

The grandmother of Jesus Christ and the mother of the Blessed Virgin Mary, St. Anne's connection to horseback riders perhaps traces, in part, to the history of her relics. In 1500, a hand-sized piece of a skull plate that had been fashioned into a full-fledged bust known as the Anna Head was stolen from St. Stephen's Church in Mainz (Rhineland, Germany) and brought to the town of Düren, near Cologne. In 1506, a papal decree allowed the stolen relic of St. Anne to remain enshrined in Düren, where annual pilgrimages were already attracting upwards of twenty thousand people. A Germanic song dating to 1516 mentions the full recovery of a Düren pilgrim from a debilitating fall from a horse as a result St. Anne's intercession.

Of greater importance is her long association with the *Confraternita dei Palafrenieri* (Confraternity of the Papal Grooms) as established by Pope Urban VI in 1378. These *palafrenieri* (modern spelling) of the papal stables made their first appearance in tenth-century records that referred to a guild of grooms who oversaw the pope's horses. These grooms held a high station at the papal court, as generally only nobility and elevated clergy could afford to keep horses, and employed only the most skillful and knowledgeable men to care for and train them. When the Confraternity was first formed, it took St. Anne as its patron and was based at the now-demolished church known as *Sant'Anna a Ripa*, then at the chapel of St. Anne at Old St. Peter's. In 1505, Pope Julius II gave this group of Rome's finest horsemen a charter known as the *Venerabile Arciconfraternita di Sant'Anna de' Parafrenieri*. For many years, the Confraternity was based at *Sant'Anna dei Palafrenieri*, a sixteenth-century parish church on the *Via Sant'Anna* in Vatican City. It is now based at the church of *Santa Caterina della Rota*, as granted by Pope Pius XI.

See also page 98.

St. James the Greater
Feast Day: July 25

St. James the Greater was one of the twelve apostles, the son of Zebedee, and the brother of St. John the Apostle. Like his brother, St. James abandoned his fishing net to follow Christ. He was one of the few to witness Jesus' transfiguration and was called "the Greater" to distinguish him from St. James the Lesser. Following the Resurrection, St. James preached the gospel in Samaria, Judea, and Spain.

St. James the Greater was the first of the apostles to suffer martyrdom, in 44 at Jerusalem. Following his death, legend states that his body was transported by an unattended, rudderless ship steered by an angel to the Iberian Peninsula. The ship approached the shoreline where a wedding was taking place. The groom was on horseback, arrayed in his wedding finery. The horse, spooked at the sight of the approaching ship, plunged blindly into the raging sea. It is said that the miraculous intervention of St. James allowed horse and rider to escape drowning. The relics of St. James were translated to Compostela, Spain, which remains one of the church's most famous pilgrimage sites. Another legend describes how, around 834, St. James (Santiago in Spanish) miraculously appeared as a warrior riding a magnificent white horse into the thick of battle to lead the Christian army to victory in their reconquest of Spain over the Moors.

See also pages 102 and 129–30.

For the Protection of Stable Hands and Grooms

St. Anne
Memorial: July 26

St. Anne's patronage of those who ride, handle, or train horses extends to those who maintain the barns and stables where the horses reside as well as to those who provide for their compassionate and skilled care.

See also page 97.

St. Marcellus I

Memorial: January 16

In 308, St. Marcellus I was charged with putting the Christian church of Rome back together as its first bishop following the persecutions of the Roman emperor Diocletian. St. Marcellus also faced the formidable task of peacefully bringing those who had abandoned the faith into full communion with the church. The tension this created spilled onto the streets of Rome, and the Roman emperor Maxentius had St. Marcellus arrested for inciting riots. He was exiled and forced to perform hard labor for nine months. He was rescued by the clergy and a Christian widow who offered her home as a church. When the church was discovered by the emperor, he mocked it by turning it into a stable and forcing the exiled bishop of Rome to care for the animals. St. Marcellus died in 310. His remains are under the altar of San Marcello al Corso in Rome.

For the Protection of Farriers and Hoof Trimmers

St. Eligius of Noyon

Memorial: December 1

St. Eligius, born in France around 590, is best known for his patronage of horses. One legend tells of a horse that had lost a shoe vigorously fighting the saint's attempts to shoe him. So great was the horse's opposition that St. Eligius believed the horse was possessed by a demon. Having great compassion for the animal, he miraculously removed the horse's foreleg, fastened a new shoe on it, and then miraculously reattached the leg to the horse. It is said among farriers that it's better to let a horse run unshod and risk hurting his hoof than to offend St. Eligius by shodding on his feast day, which is deemed among metalsmiths the equivalent of a high holy day!

See also pages 23–24, 44, 101, and 132.

For the Protection of Saddlemakers

Sts. Crispinian and Crispin
Memorial: October 25

Third-century noblemen and evangelizers of Gaul, these brothers were shoe-makers and street preachers of Christianity. They were martyred in 286 in Rome. In the sixth century, a church was built in their honor in Soissons, France, which had been the seat of their ministry. There is a natural connection as patrons of saddlemakers via their profession (leather shoemaking). In addition, a plaque of the great patron saint of horses, St. Eligius, is prominently displayed in the Soissons shrine, which supports how they have been adopted by saddlemakers as patron saints. The saintly brothers are often depicted with the tools of their trade or holding strips of leather.

St. Gualfardus of Augsburg
Memorial: April 30

Born in 1070 in Augsburg, Germany, and a master harness maker by trade, St. Gualfardus set off on a pilgrimage in 1096 that brought him through Verona, Italy. He stayed there for some time, turning out some very fine saddles. He gave the proceeds to the sick and the poor before setting out for the nearby forest where he would live as a hermit for twenty years. Some accounts say he then returned to city life and reopened his shop for a time, while others have him leaving the wilderness for an austere cell adjoining a church. In either case, he was known for his piety, compassion, and fasting, and was widely sought for his healing miracles. At the time of his death in 1127, he was a Camaldolese Benedictine monk in residence at a priory near Verona. He is also recognized as the patron saint of harness makers.

St. Paul the Apostle
Memorial: June 29

A first-century Pharisee, contemporary of the apostles, and a tentmaker by trade, St. Paul, as Saul of Tarsus, was known for his early persecution of Christians. Although he took a prominent role in the stoning of St. Stephen, the first martyr for the faith, he experienced a profound conversion and became an evangelist who would change the world. However, even after his conversion, he continued to practice his trade as a tentmaker to earn his keep as an itinerant teacher and preacher. His skill with leather-making tools likely led saddlemakers to adopt St. Paul as their patron. He was martyred in 67 in Rome.

See also pages 17 and 186.

For the Protection of Veterinarians

St. Blaise
Memorial: February 3
St. Blaise was a fourth-century Armenian bishop of Sebastea as well as a physician. He became well known for his association with a blessing that heals the throat: *Per intercessionem Sancti Blasii liberet te Deus a malo gutteris et a quovis alio malo.* ("May God at the intercession of St. Blaise preserve you from troubles of the throat and every other evil.") His tender care and healing abilities extended to people and animals alike. Not surprisingly, then, in some farming regions, water consecrated with this same blessing is given to sick cattle.

See also pages 5, 52, 59, and 126.

St. Eligius of Noyon
Memorial: December 1
Given his patronage for protection against equine diseases, which arose both from the miraculous cure of a sick horse through his intercession as well as his patronage of horses in general, it became fitting for the faithful to entrust to him the veterinary care of all animals.

See also pages 23–24, 44, 99, and 132.

St. James the Greater
Memorial: July 25

St. James's patronage of horses and equestrians likely led those riders whose lives often depended on their horses to invoke his aid in keeping their mounts healthy and strong—performing, in essence, the work of a veterinarian.

See also pages 98 and 129–30.

For the Protection of Gardeners

St. Abdon and St. Sennen
Memorial: July 30

These two Persian noblemen and brothers, who were secretly Christians, were arrested for using their own estate for the compassionate burial of Christian martyrs. They were brought to Rome, where they were cast into an arena with bears and lions, all of which refused to harm them. They were martyred in 253 at the hands of gladiators.

Their association with gardeners may stem in part from a liturgical prayer invoking their names: "Hearken to our earnest prayers, O blessed martyrs! May the faith at length triumph in that land of Persia whence so many flowers have been culled for heaven."

Another legend states that when a region in France known as Arles was overrun with criminals who descended from the Pyrenees mountains with the intention of pillaging the villages, terrorizing the people, and destroying the crops, the abbot of Arles, St. Arnulph, set off for Rome to secure a holy relic that might restore peace, prosperity, and fertility to the land. Led in a dream to the burial place of the two Persian saints (led, in fact, by the saints themselves!), he returned to Arles with the powerful relics of St. Abdon and St. Sennen. The relics were transported in a liquor barrel filled with holy water that, once poured into an empty sarcophagus, became an inexhaustible source of healing miracles. The land was healed, and the water at Arles-sur-Tech continues to miraculously flow from the sarcophagus, producing two hundred liters per year of pure water, which is collected by the Benedictines at the Abbey of Saint Mary at Arles-sur-Tech, where the relics reside, and then dispensed to the faithful. Gardens and crops sprinkled with this blessed water have thrived under the patronage of these saintly brothers.

Adam the Patriarch
Memorial: December 24

Adam is the Old Testament Patriarch and father of the human race. He lived in the Garden of Eden until he was banished from there by God. His name is associated in Genesis 2:7 with the word *ha-adamah* ("the ground"). According to one tradition, following Adam's expulsion from the Garden of Eden, the angel Gabriel gave him wheat-grains and various agricultural instruments and taught him how to work the land in such a way that he and his family would find sustenance. Though not formally canonized, Adam's intercession as the first human being created and loved by God, and someone who lived in a garden, gives hope to farmers and gardeners alike!

St. Adelard of Corbie
Memorial: January 2

A cousin of Charlemagne and nobleman by birth, in 773, St. Adelard turned his back on the comforts of the royal court to become a Benedictine monk. He resided at Corbie Abbey in Picardy, France, where he was a contemplative gardener as well as an advisor to Charlemagne. He was exiled in 817 after being charged with supporting a revolt against Charlemagne's successor, the emperor Louis the Debonair. St. Adelard was known for supreme humility and devoted care of the poor. He died in 827 of natural causes. He is often depicted as an abbot digging in a garden with a crown nearby.

St. Agnes of Rome
Memorial: January 21

The name *Agnes* means "chaste, lamb, pure one." Because of her devotion to Christ, St. Agnes fiercely resisted the hand in marriage of a nobleman who expected her to sacrifice to pagan gods. When led to the altar of the Roman goddess Minerva, the twelve-year-old defiantly made the sign of the cross and was summarily tortured. She was offered last-minute marriage proposals by several men but chose martyrdom instead. She was beheaded (or stabbed or burned, depending on various accounts of her death) in January of 254 (alternately, 304) in Rome. Her body was received by her noble parents and buried in a field they owned outside of Rome; it may be inferred from this that they were wealthy landowners who leased out their fields for farming.

Her loose association with growing things can be traced to the Eve of St. Agnes (January 20), which was celebrated in medieval times as a special night when an unmarried woman was said to dream of her future husband, provided she carried out a series of rituals. One such ritual was particular to Scotland, where Scottish girls would meet in a field at midnight, throw grain onto the soil and pray:

> Agnes sweet and Agnes fair,
> Hither, hither, now repair;
> Bonny Agnes, let me see
> The lad who is to marry me.

The dainty white flower commonly known as the spring snowflake (*Leucojum aestivum*), native to central and southern Europe, is often referred to as St. Agnes's flower owing to its loveliness and stark white purity. Another St. Agnes flower is the traditional Christmas rose, with its pure white blossoms.

See also page 143.

St. Christopher
Memorial: July 25

St. Christopher was said to have once been a heathen Canaanite named Reprobus, a man who was exceedingly large and powerfully strong, a fearsome giant who set out to find and serve the most powerful master on earth. His quest led him to a king who employed Reprobus as his personal bodyguard. However, when the name of Satan was invoked and the king cowered, Reprobus set out to find Satan, whom he found in the dark of the forest. He was accepted into the dark prince's service, but when he saw Satan running from the sight of a crucifix planted by the wayside, Reprobus was inspired to search for Jesus Christ, whom he now understood to be the most powerful being in heaven and on earth. Finding a hermit who knew and served Christ, Reprobus received instruction in the Christian way and was baptized in a high, swiftly running river. The hermit suggested that Reprobus use his size and strength to carry on his broad shoulders wayfarers who needed to cross the river, and he performed this task day and night.

One day, hearing the cries of a child, St. Christopher rushed to his assistance. But, having placed the boy on his shoulders and taking his staff in hand, he was quickly surprised by the crushing weight of the child. In giving voice to his despair over the "weight of the world," the Child revealed himself to be Jesus Christ.

Jesus re-christened Reprobus with the name *Christophorus*, which means Christ Bearer, and instructed Christophorus to plant his staff in the ground when he reached the other side of the river, promising that it would burst forth with leaves and blossoms as a sign of Jesus' divine presence. At that, the Christ child disappeared, and the staff of St. Christopher burst into bloom. St. Christopher became a most effective missionary preacher who converted many thousands of souls. For this, he was imprisoned, tortured, and, on July 25, 254, under the rule of the Roman emperor Decius, beheaded.

See also pages 132 and 182.

St. Dorothy of Caesarea
Memorial: February 6

Often depicted as a maiden carrying a basket of fruit and flowers, or crowned with a wreath of roses, St. Dorothy was a virgin martyr who refused to sacrifice to pagan idols. At the time of her martyrdom in modern-day Turkey in 303, she was mocked by a student of the law named Theophilus, who asked if she would kindly send him roses from that so-called paradise where she professed to be going. St. Dorothy made a promise to do so, and following her beheading, "a fair child barefoot and clothed in purple with crisp hairs, whose garment was set full of bright stars" appeared to Theophilus shortly thereafter in the emperor's palace. The child handed him three apples and three roses from a golden basket, professing to have come to him at the request of the Christian martyr Dorothy. The child, said to be an angel, then disappeared. Given that it was the middle of winter, Theophilus was astonished. He was converted on the spot and himself went on to suffer martyrdom. St. Dorothy's body was taken to Rome, and every year on her feast day, apples and roses are blessed at the church there that bears her name. She is also the patroness of flowers, especially roses.

St. Fiacre
Memorial: September 1

Born around 600, St. Fiacre was raised in an Irish monastery known for its scholarship. He was instructed in the use of healing herbs, which he greatly enjoyed. His vast knowledge, skill, and priestly holiness attracted many admirers, which interrupted the holy solitude he craved. He fled to France, to the region of Brie, and upon establishing a hermitage in a cave near a spring, acquired the admiration and patronage of the good bishop St. Faro of Meaux. St. Fiacre asked for land for a garden to grow food and healing herbs. In reply, the bishop said he could have as much land around the hermitage as he could entrench in one day. Early the next morning, St. Fiacre walked the perimeter of the plot of land he desired, dragging his ivory staff behind him. The staff miraculously razed trees, uprooted bushes, and flattened the dense, stemmy brush with tremendous speed and efficiency. At the end of the day, the bishop surveyed the clear-cut land and declared the feat a miracle. St. Fiacre then cultivated a garden that pilgrims flocked to for centuries thereafter.

St. Fiacre was also well known for working miraculous healings through the laying on of hands. He constructed an oratory in honor of the Blessed Virgin and a hospice for strangers. He died in 670 of natural causes and is particularly invoked for the successful gardening of herbs and vegetables. He is often depicted with a spade in hand, looking tenderly at the ground where he will turn the earth and produce a bountiful harvest. In addition to his patronage of gardeners, he has been unofficially adopted as the patron saint of herbalists.

St. Gertrude of Nivelles
Memorial: March 17

The daughter of powerful nobility, St. Gertrude of Nivelles was born around 626 in what is now Belgium. After rejecting the notion of marriage, she became, at the age of twenty, the abbess of a Benedictine monastery in Nivelles that had been founded by her mother. At the monastery, St. Gertrude kept a lovely garden and exercised a special devotion to praying for the souls in purgatory. Several years later, she entrusted the care of the monastery to a few capable nuns in order to spend more time reading and studying sacred Scripture. A visionary and an ascetic, she died on March 17, 657, at the age of thirty-three, some say as a result of her overly harsh penitential practices. Folklore held that good weather on her feast day indicated that it was the right time to begin spring planting.

See also pages 13 and 37.

St. Phocas the Gardener
Memorial: July 3 (alternately, also July 23 and September 22)

A humble farmer, innkeeper, and gardener, St. Phocas was known for using his surplus crops to feed the local poor, which he did in the name of Christ. He was beheaded in 303 in Sinope, Pontus (modern-day Turkey) by two Roman soldiers. Many miracles took place at the site of his burial, and a church that houses his relics was later constructed there. He is often depicted in art holding a shovel or surrounded by a harvest of produce.

See also pages 17–18 and 82.

St. Rose of Lima
Memorial: August 23

The first saint born in the Americas, in 1586, St. Rose of Lima was the daughter of a Spanish father and Peruvian mother who christened her Isabel. At her confirmation, she took the name of Rose because it was said that as an infant in the cradle, her face had been kissed by a mystical, hovering rose. Alternately, it was said she was nicknamed Rose at an early age because of her perpetually rosy cheeks. Either way, she grew up to be a beautiful, chaste girl who deliberately marred her lovely complexion by applying pepper and lye to her face before going out in public. She lived and prayed in a small grotto that included a flower and vegetable garden, and embroidered items to sell for the benefit of her family and the local poor. It was said that the roses she cultivated, some of which bloomed out of season, were of the most extraordinary color and fragrance. She became a Third Order Dominican, she was a mystic who received invisible stigmata, and she was an ascetic who practiced severe mortifications. She died in 1617 of natural causes and was canonized in 1671.

St. Serenus the Gardener
Memorial: February 23

Wishing only to live a quiet life of prayer and solitude, St. Serenus left his home in Greece to live as a hermit in Sirmiun, Pannonia (Hungary). He kept a fruit and herb garden, which he labored over with great diligence even as his thoughts turned to God. In the heat of the day, he discovered a finely dressed woman and her daughters meandering through the garden. Mindful of the heat and her well-to-do appearance, he gently suggested they come back in the evening, when it was cooler. The woman took his suggestion as a reprimand and promptly reported the gardener's insolence to her husband, who was a member of Emperor Maximian's imperial guard. St. Serenus was arrested, but was acquitted of wrongdoing at his trial. However, his kind, gentle demeanor gave rise to accusations that he was a Christian. St. Serenus admitted it was so, and was ordered by the judge to renounce his faith and make a sacrifice to pagan gods. When St. Serenus refused, he was sentenced to death. He was martyred in February of 303.

St. Tryphon of Lampsacus
Memorial: February 1

Born around 222 in Phrygia (modern-day Turkey), St. Tryphon was raised in a Christian family. His gifts of oration and teaching brought about many conversions, for which he was martyred in Nicaea in 251 during the Roman emperor Decius's persecutions. Given that his prayers were known to have turned back a plague of crop-destroying locusts from the fields in his village, he was later adopted as a patron saint by those seeking help in banishing pests from their gardens. It was also said that when his relics were translated from his native land back to Nicaea, lilies bloomed out of season on his feast day of February 1.

See also pages 12 and 63.

St. Werenfridus
Memorial: August 14

Born in eighth-century England and predominately known as the patron saint of vegetable gardeners, St. Werenfridus was a Benedictine monk in Ireland, was ordained to the priesthood, and then sent forth as a missionary. He evangelized the Frisians and Saxons with great zeal, especially within the territory of Batavia in Holland. During his years as a Benedictine monk, he cared for the monastery garden, providing food for his community as well as for the local peasants in need. When he died in 780, the fragrance of roses and lilies arose from his gravesite. Pilgrims to his tomb in Elst in the Netherlands have received the benefit of many miraculous cures, particularly of gout.

For the Protection of Flower Growers

St. Thérèse of Lisieux
Memorial: October 1

Born in 1873 in Alencon (Normandy, France) and christened Marie-Francoise Thérèse Martin, St. Thérèse, popularly known as the Little Flower, suffered the loss of her saintly Catholic mother when she was four years old. Her devout father moved his five daughters (all of whom would become nuns) to Lisieux, France. There, she was educated by Benedictine nuns, showing great faith from an early age. At the age of fourteen, she petitioned to join the

Carmelites, who turned her down because of her young age. She was not to be dissuaded. She took her petition all the way to Rome, and was admitted to the religious order of Carmelites at Lisieux at the age of fifteen. She made her final vows two years later.

In her short lifetime, St. Thérèse suffered greatly from tuberculosis. She received many graces and consolations in prayer and endured bouts of spiritual darkness. Lucky for us, she was ordered by her wise prioress to keep a journal of her thoughts, memories, and the experiences of her faith journey. This journal became the beautiful autobiography *Story of a Soul.*

For St. Thérèse, the shortest and most direct path to heaven consisted of childlike love, simplicity, and unconditional trust in God. This recipe for how to live is known as The Little Way. Having no capacity in her daily life to perform great deeds, she chose instead to do small things with great love.

As she lay dying from tuberculosis in the infirmary, she could see through the window the splendor of the rose bushes in bloom. She had always loved roses, and recalled having scattered them before the Blessed Sacrament when she was a child. She died in 1897 at the age of twenty-four, but before dying she proclaimed, "After my death, I will let fall a shower of roses. . . . I feel my mission is about to begin, my mission to make God loved as I love him, of giving my little way to souls." St. Thérèse was canonized in 1925 and declared a doctor of the church by Pope St. John Paul II in 1997.

For the Protection of Grain Merchants

St. Nicholas of Myra
Memorial: December 6

As archbishop of Myra, St. Nicholas was able to alleviate the suffering caused by a terrible famine that came over the region. He convinced sailors delivering a shipment of grain to the emperor that if they shared a portion with him, their delivery would not show any diminishment, as indeed it did not. St. Nicholas distributed the grain, and the people were miraculously sustained by the grain for two years.

See also pages 80–81, 88–89, 114, 121, 125, 133–34, and 182.

For the Protection of Harvesters

St. Peter the Apostle
Memorial: June 29

A first-century fisherman from Galilee who was called by Jesus Christ to leave his nets to become a fisher of men, Simon Peter was one of the twelve apostles and the one to whom Jesus entrusted the keys to the kingdom of heaven. As both a zealous teacher and bold preacher, writer of two canonical epistles, and the first bishop of Rome, he converted thousands to the Christian faith in glorious imitation of Jesus, the Lord and Master of the Harvest. As the "rock" upon which Christ was to build his church, St. Peter preached the gospel until his martyrdom by way of the cross in Rome in 67. His association as the patron saint of harvesters who pray for abundance in their fields likely stems from the allegorical language used in Matthew 9:35–38. In producing a bountiful harvest of souls, St. Peter did not disappoint!

See also page 89.

For the Protection of Haymakers

Sts. Gervase and Protase
Memorial: June 19

Sts. Gervase and Protase were twin brothers born in the second century to Sts. Vitalis and Valeria, both of whom were martyred for the faith. After the death of their parents, the brothers sold their worldly goods and isolated themselves in a small cell in Milan, Italy. Here, they prayed and secretly studied sacred Scripture for nearly ten years before being discovered. They were martyred under the persecutions of the Roman emperor Nero. In 368, the location of their buried bodies was revealed in a dream to St. Ambrose, bishop of Milan, just as he completed the construction of Milan's basilica. It was there that the relics of Sts. Gervase and Protase were joyously translated.

While little is known about the lives of these two saints, they are widely venerated by farmers in Germany and parts of France. A German saying ("peasant rule") amongst hay harvesters is, *Wenn's regnet auf Gervasius / es vierzig Tage regnen muss.* ("When it rains on St. Gervasius's Day / forty days of rain will follow.") For haymakers in America, the first cutting of the season's grass takes place around mid-June. The hay farmer will pray for enough rain to make the grass grow, but not so much that it will make the grass hay—which is essential food for many farm animals—too wet to cut and gather. Centuries ago, before modern machinery, it would take several days for a farmer to cut, dry, and collect the hay, as most of the cutting work was done with handheld scythes. Since hay gets destroyed if it becomes too wet, the farmers used to pray for a series of dry days to facilitate the cutting and gathering of the hay. One can presume that St. Gervase was invoked on his feast day to keep the forty days of rain at bay.

Patrons of Seed, Flour, and Spice Merchants

From "loaves and fishes" to buttermilk biscuits,
bread in all its forms and flavors is a vital part of life.
These saints of the pantry help those who work
to keep our cupboards filled and deliver us our daily bread.

St. Honorius of Amiens
Memorial: May 16

Born near Amiens, France, to a noble family in the mid-seventh century, St. Honorius was instructed in the faith by St. Beatus, the bishop of Amiens. St. Honorius reluctantly assumed the bishopric of Amiens; at his election, holy oil was said to miraculously appear on his head. So astonished was his former nursemaid to learn he had been proclaimed a bishop, she remarked she would only believe the news if the peel (that is, the oven shovel) she was using to bake bread turned itself into a tree. The peel was placed in the ground, sprouted roots, and turned into a magnificent mulberry tree. This story gave rise to the saint's widespread patronage of bakers, whose reliance on grains for their pastries led to the association of St. Honorius as the patron saint of seed merchants ("corn chandlers") as well. In those times, a corn chandler was a person who supplied grain and corn. Corn was the generic name for wheat, barley, and oats, not simply maize as it is defined today. In 1202, a wealthy baker donated some land in Paris to build a chapel dedicated to the saint, and in 1400, Parisian bakers established their guild in the church of St. Honoratus. It is said that when his body was exhumed in 1060, his relics were the catalyst for many miracles.

For the Protection of Spice Merchants

St. Nicholas of Myra
Memorial: December 6

Growers of crops such as chili pepper, saffron, garlic, sesame seeds, ginger, and other spices have a patron in St. Nicholas of Myra. Many legends spread about St. Nicholas and his generosity to the poor, but the one that greatly forged his identity as "Santa Claus" stems from assistance he provided to a wealthy spice merchant named Dimitri. Having lost his trading ships in a series of calamities including shipwreck, piracy, and fire, Dimitri went from being one of Myra's wealthiest merchants to being penniless. In desperation, he contemplated prostituting his three daughters so that the family could survive. Upon receiving news of the merchant's fate, St. Nicholas discreetly visited his house at night and threw three bags of gold coins through the window, thereby saving his daughters from a cruel and sordid fate. Having discovered that the family's benefactor was St. Nicholas, Dimitri fell prostrate before him in gratitude. It is said that the saint silenced him by telling him to thank *God*, who had left him with the fortune; he was merely following Jesus' command to share with those in need.

Having the necessary dowries, Dimitri gave each of his daughters in marriage to chivalrous suitors. Over time, he was able to acquire more ships and restore his business and worldly wealth, much of which he often secretly left in the back of the church for St. Nicholas to share with others.

See also pages 80–81, 88–89, 110–11, 121, 125, 133–34, and 182.

For the Protection of Hop Pickers

St. Arnulf of Soissons
Memorial: July 18

Born of the noble class in Flanders, Belgium, in 1040, the early part of St. Arnulf's life was spent in military service to Kings Robert and Henry I. In 1060, he entered the Benedictine monastery of St. Medard in Soissons, France, and obtained the abbot's permission to reside in a small cell, where he lived a prayerful and penitential life for three years. He was summoned to succeed the abbot, which he did with reluctance. Despite his preference for solitude, he was chosen to become the bishop of Soissons in 1081, an office he retained for fewer than two years before he was ousted by an intruder. Rather than fight for the office, he retired once more, this time to an abbey he founded, the Abbey of St. Peter in Oudenburg (Flanders, now Belgium), where he began to brew beer. He exhorted the local villagers to drink beer instead of the water, maintaining it was healthier than the contaminated water found in the local wells. Given that the water that made the beer was boiled, it was free from contaminants and indeed provided the gift of health, particularly during the time of the plague. It was a type of beer called "small beer," which had a relatively low alcohol content and could even be consumed at breakfast.

In 1087, St. Arnulf died a humble, penitent monk wearing sackcloth and ashes. He is sometimes represented in art as a bishop holding a mash rake, which is a tool of the brewing trade.

For the Protection of Tobacconists

St. Catherine dé Ricci
Memorial: February 13
Alexandra de' Ricci was born on April 23, 1522, to a socially prominent family of wealthy bankers and merchants in Florence, Italy. Her mother died during her infancy, but she was raised by a loving father and stepmother. She was also cared for by her uncle, who served as priest and confessor for the Dominican nuns at the Convent of San Vincenzo Ferrer in nearby Prato. After many trials, her father finally relented and allowed her to enter that same Dominican convent at the age of twelve, and she took the religious name Catherine. She had many mystical experiences, including bilocation, and at the age of twenty she experienced the sacred stigmata and weekly ecstasies of the Passion, which

lasted for twenty-eight consecutive hours over the course of twelve years. Even amid these mystical experiences and severe penitential practices, St. Catherine served as prioress of her convent for thirty-six years and was a widely sought out spiritual advisor to prominent families in Florence. As a superior, she was kind, considerate, and cheerful, and exercised a particular dedication to caring for the sick and infirm. She died on February 2, 1590. She was declared a saint in 1746, and her incorrupt remains are venerated in the *Basilica of San Vincenzo e Santa Caterina de' Ricci*, which is attached to the saint's original convent.

It is said that when she experienced the sacred stigmata, especially at her death, her Passion wounds, including everything she touched, exuded a fragrance of sweetness and sanctity. Perhaps her Passion wounds released the lovely fragrances of roses or tobacco flowers, which would explain her attribution as the patroness of tobacconists. An alternate explanation is that the city of Florence had long enjoyed a connection with the tobacco industry. In 1561, Jean Nicot (from which is derived the word *nicotine*), then French ambassador to Portugal, encountered "tabaco" in his travels. He brought the seeds to the queen of France, Catherine de' Medici, in Florence, and cited its medicinal properties. It is said that Catherine de' Medici and her son Francis II soothed their migraine headaches with the plant, and the entire court thus adopted this "queen's herb." The queen's bishop obtained some of the seeds and shared them with his uncle, the bishop of San Sepolcro, which is a town located in the region of Tuscany. San Sepolcro became the center for tobacco plant cultivation. The leaves were shipped to Florence, where cigars were made. The famous Tuscan cigar was accidentally created in 1815 when tobacco leaves shipped to Florence were left out in a rainstorm, and they were soaked through. Rather than throwing them away the foreman decided he would try drying them. This resulted in a second fermentation that produced a peculiar-tasting tobacco that was embraced by the Tuscans. It is likely that the Tuscan tobacconists adopted St. Catherine as their patron saint given her local prominence and veneration as a powerful saint throughout the region.

For the Protection of Vine Dressers

St. Urban of Langres
Memorial: April 2

Consecrated as the bishop of Langres, France, in 374, St. Urban is honored in parts of Burgundy and the surrounding region as the patron saint of vinedressers and gardeners. Soon after his ordination as bishop, he was swept up in political turmoil, forcing him to hide from his persecutors in a vineyard. The local vinedressers concealed him, and, in turn, the bishop evangelized among them. As the number of converts grew, they assisted St. Urban in his ministries as he moved between towns and vineyards. He was beloved by all those who labored in vineyards, and he was known for working miracles among them. He died in 390 of natural causes.

See also page 161.

For the Protection of Vintners

St. Amand of Maastricht
Memorial: February 6

St. Amand was no stranger to adversity. He had become a hermit and a monk by the age of twenty. His wealthy family, thinking he had lost his mind for having so great a devotion to Christ, tried to kidnap him. He was commissioned as a missionary preacher to evangelize throughout France, Flanders, and Germany, but received frequent beatings by hostile locals. In 649, he became the bishop of Maastricht, in the Netherlands. In his lifetime, he founded several monasteries and convents. His missionary preaching often brought him through parts of Europe well known for brewing beer and making wine. Over time, he was adopted as a patron saint by workers in these professions. He died in 676 at the age of ninety.

See also page 133.

St. Donatus of Munstereifel
Memorial: June 30

St. Donatus was born in Rome in the second century to a Christian mother, Flaminia, and a pagan father named Faustus. He was the wonder child whose birth was predicted by St. Gervase, and it was St. Gervase's prayers that healed Faustus on his deathbed.

Having been educated in the Christian faith, St. Donatus enlisted in the famed Twelfth Legion *Fulminata* ("Thundering Legion"), where he served as a personal bodyguard to Marcus Aurelius. In 173, the legion was caught up in a terrible battle in Moravia, along the Danube River. Just as they were on the verge of being overcome, St. Donatus rallied the legion, praying for deliverance. At that moment, a miraculous thunderstorm arose that was so fierce, it drove back the enemy. St. Donatus openly proclaimed his thanks to God, and was martyred for professing his Christian faith. Other accounts have him exposed as a Christian when he refused to marry the emperor's granddaughter.

As the patron against lightning strikes, he is often linked with St. Florian, who protects against fire and floods. Together, particularly in Hungary in the Balaton wine region, the saints are dually invoked to protect the wine harvest, and therefore the wine makers as well. He is often depicted wearing the armor of a Roman soldier, armed with a thunderbolt, and holding a palm or a grapevine.

See also page 170.

St. Goar of Aquitaine
Memorial: July 6

St. Goar was a young clergyman from Aquitaine, France. He embraced the life of a hermit by taking up residence in a cave on the banks of the Rhine River in Germany. He also served as a missionary to the locals, and gave pastoral care to the Rhine boatmen. He was known to recite the entire Psalter after offering Mass. In his later years, he was offered the role of bishop of Triers, which he refused. Many legends and accounts of miracles arose after his death in 575, and his grave became a pilgrimage site. The town and church of Sankt

Goar were built in his honor near his hermitage and grave. In 1240, noble-men planted vineyards that produced primarily Riesling in Sankt Goar, on the terraced slopes of the Rhine. Winemakers in the region look to the miracle worker St. Goar for protection and favorable harvests.

St. John the Apostle
Memorial: December 27

There is a legend that St. John survived drinking a glass of poisoned wine offered to him by a pagan priest of Ephesus because he blessed the wine first. This miracle confirmed the Scripture that foretold, "These signs will accompany those who believe: in my name they will cast out demons, they will speak new languages. They will pick up serpents [with their hands], and if they drink any deadly thing, it will not harm them; they will lay hands on the sick, and they will recover" (Mark 16:17–18). The wine of St. John is also said to be symbolic of the deep love and unity he shared with Christ. As late as the mid-twentieth century, Catholics in Central Europe brought cider and wine to the local church on St. John's feast day to be blessed or sprinkled with holy water by a priest. Afterward, the family took the blessed wine home and poured some of it into every barrel.

Traditionally, following the main course, St. John's wine, often called St. John's Love, was given by sips to each family member, including small chil-dren. The ritual was enacted by the head of the household handing out each glass and saying, "I drink thee the love of St. John." The partaker replied, "I thank thee for the love of St. John."

See also pages 87, 147, and 186.

St. Lawrence
Memorial: August 10

An archdeacon of Rome in the mid-third century, St. Lawrence was martyred in 258 by being grilled over gridirons. This accounts for his patronage of cooks and those who work in or supply kitchens. One might say that he is the patron saint, then, of all things gastronomic, which naturally includes wine.

On St. Lawrence Day, feasts are held throughout the city of Rome, many of which include gourmet food and wine pairings. His feast day falls near the harvesting of grapes, which happens on the heels of the church's blessing of the grapes, a tradition that takes place on the Feast of the Transfiguration (August 6). St. Lawrence's duties also included safeguarding relics housed in Rome, among them the Holy Chalice in Valencia (one of four cups believed to be those from which Jesus and his apostles drank consecrated wine at the Last Supper). St. Lawrence had given the Holy Chalice to a loyal Christian soldier to take to the saint's homeland in Spain, in present-day Aragon, before his impending arrest.

St. Lawrence also has a connection to brewers because something like a gridiron can be used in drying hops or malt. The brewer's guild in Bamberg, Germany, adopted him as a patron saint; apprentices were required to carry his image in processions and to make donations to the local church that bore his name.

See also pages 87–88 and 181.

St. Martin of Tours
Memorial: November 12
St. Martin's feast day on November 11 corresponds with the annual festival throughout parts of Europe called St. Martin's Day (Martinmas), which celebrates the drinking of the first wine of the season and coincides with what was historically the feast day of Bacchus, the Roman god of wine. Gradually, the Christian church assimilated the pagan feast day, and those who were employed in the vineyards took St. Martin as their patron saint.

See also pages 48–49 and 66.

St. Morand of Cluny
Memorial: June 3
A Benedictine monk and priest who was born to a noble family in Germany, St. Morand was known for his sanctity, his miracles, and his founding of a monastery in Altkirch, France. It is said that St. Morand lived the entire period of Lent sustained by one cluster of grapes, thus making him the patron of both winemakers and growers of grapes.

See also page 225 for the Blessing of Grapes.

St. Nicholas of Myra
Memorial: December 6

The miracles performed by St. Nicholas during his lifetime continued long after his death. As one legend goes, the people of Myra were celebrating the saint on the eve of his feast day when a band of Arab pirates infiltrated the town. They absconded with the treasures of the Church of St. Nicholas and kidnapped a young boy, Basilios, to sell as a slave in Crete. The ruler of Crete chose Basilios to be his personal cupbearer, as he could speak freely without the risk of his foreign words being understood or repeated by Basilios. For the next year, Basilios performed his sole duty of serving the ruler wine in a golden cup. When the following feast day of St. Nicholas came to pass, his grieving mother refused to join in the festivities and spent the day in prayer for the return of her beloved son. Her prayers were heard, and it is said that St. Nicholas suddenly appeared to Basilios as he held a golden cup filled with choice wine, whisked the boy away, and set him safely before his parents, with the golden cup of wine still clenched in his small hands.

See also pages 80–81, 88–89, 110–11, 114, 125, 133–34, and 182.

St. Tychon of Amathus
Memorial: June 16

Born to a poor family of bakers in Cyprus in the fifth century, St. Tychon was schooled in Scripture from a young age and was known to have the gift of wonder working as a child. He often gave away to the poor the bread his father had baked. Nevertheless, the family's store of grain never ran out. Legend tells of the saint's possession of a dried-up vine from a spent vineyard, which he planted and prayed over, asking the Lord that the vine might take root and yield fruit for the health of the people. A vineyard that supplied plentiful grapes for the wine used during Holy Mass, its yield lasting throughout St. Tychon's lifetime and beyond, sprang up from that one vine. When he became the bishop of Amathus, Cyprus, St. Tychon dedicated himself to ridding the island of paganism, and in particular the worship of Aphrodite. He also dedicated himself to the care and service of the poor. He foretold the time of his own death, which came to pass as he had predicted, in 425.

St. Vincent of Saragossa
Memorial: January 22

Born in Aragon, Spain, St. Vincent was a deacon to St. Valerius of Saragossa, also in Spain, and was imprisoned during the persecutions of the Roman emperor Diocletian in the early-fourth century. He was tortured on a rack (some accounts say a wine-press chest) but was offered clemency by the governor Dacian if he would relinquish his books of sacred Scripture to be burned. He refused. He was tortured on a gridiron, then thrown into prison, where he was visited and ministered to by angels. St. Vincent's praise of God amid such suffering so astonished his prison guard, he immediately converted. St. Vincent's body was thrown into a field, where it was expected that it would be devoured by birds and beasts. Angels kept guard, and a raven protected the body with its wings until his body was fastened to a millstone and tossed into the sea, where it miraculously preceded the sailors who disposed of it back to the shoreline. The saint's remains were claimed on the shore by a pious woman who brought them to a small chapel outside of Valencia, whereupon many miracles began to occur.

St. Vincent's patronage of vintners stems in part from a belief in the Burgundy region of France that invoking his name will protect vineyards from the frost that is known to occur on or near his feast day. In other areas of Europe, his feast day marks the restful time of year when winemakers gather to assess the merits of the previous year's vintage, as well as to honor the saint with celebrations and Masses. Other associations include a sixth-century Benedictine abbey which was dedicated to St. Vincent and the Holy Cross. There, monks planted and tended a vineyard that was placed under the protection of St. Vincent.

For the Protection of Distillers

St. Louis IX
Memorial: August 25

The king of France from age eleven in 1226 until he died in 1270, St. Louis, a chivalrous, devout, and charitable Christian, was known as a reformer of the

French judicial system. He was also a fearless warrior and staunch supporter of the church. He founded monasteries, aided religious orders, built hospitals, and obtained relics for the edification of France, including the Crown of Thorns and a large piece of the True Cross, which served as a healing remedy in 1244 when he was stricken with a deadly fever. Having miraculously recovered, he led a crusade to Egypt, where he was captured and then ransomed in 1250. He returned to France, but that didn't deter him from heading off to lead a second crusade in 1270, a crusade from which he did not return, having been stricken with typhoid fever almost immediately upon arriving in Tunis. He died on August 25, 1270.

St. Louis is the only French monarch ever canonized. St. Louis Cathedral in New Orleans and the city of St. Louis, Missouri, were named in his honor. He is the patron saint of both cities, which have long served as centers for the distilling of beer and a variety of spirits. Naturally, distillers in these areas adopted the patron of their cities as the patron of their livelihood as well.

St. Mary–the Nativity of the Blessed Virgin
Memorial: September 8

Mary, mother of God, whose nativity is celebrated on September 8, was born to an elderly couple, Anne and Joachim. She was conceived without sin as a grace from God, who had chosen Mary to become the mother of his Son, Jesus. The memorial originated with the consecration on that day of a sixth-century church built in Jerusalem under the patronage of St. Helen, Constantine's mother, and known as the Basilica of St. Anne. By the seventh century, the memorial was celebrated in Rome, and subsequently spread throughout the Western church over the course of the next two centuries. Distillers of spirits may have taken a page from the book of French winemakers, who discovered the intercessory power of Our Lady to preserve and protect their livelihood. In the Rhone region of France, a gothic church called *La Chapelle Notre-Dame-aux-Raisins* (translated "Our Lady of the Grapes") looms from the summit of Mount Brouilly. Located in the Beaujolais wine area, the church was erected in the wake of a devastating harvest mildew that lasted from 1850 to 1852. The vintners, seeking Our Lady's favor and intercession in healing their land, built a church in her honor that was inaugurated on the feast day of the

Nativity of the Blessed Virgin in 1857 and is a day of great celebration for wine-makers throughout France even in modern times. Winemakers make a pilgrimage to the top of the mountain with their best grapes from the early harvest, where the grapes are blessed and placed into the hands of a statue of Mary.

See also pages 145 and 149–50.

For the Protection of Spinners

St. Catherine of Alexandria
Memorial: November 25

Having received a very fine intellectual formation thanks to her noble birth in Alexandria, Egypt, St. Catherine of Alexandria, who converted at the age of eighteen, is said to have vigorously debated the pagan philosophers of her time as to the absolute truth of Christianity. Many of these pagans were converted by her arguments. She was martyred under the persecutions of the Roman emperor Maximian, who had her scourged and tossed into prison as punishment for her relentless evangelization. However, having been impressed by her preaching and convictions, the emperor's wife, accompanied by the leader of Maximian's army, went to visit St. Catherine in her cell. Both of them were converted and martyred.

The enraged emperor ordered St. Catherine to be strapped to the breaking wheel so that her body would be shattered to pieces, but as soon as St. Catherine met the instrument of torture, it splintered into flying debris that caused the death of many of the spectators. By virtue of this association with the breaking wheel, spinners of wool, whose work uses a wheel and treadle, embrace her as their patron saint. St. Catherine was beheaded in 305. It is said that angels carried her body to Mount Sinai, where healing oil flows from her tomb. St. Catherine of Alexandria is one of the Fourteen Holy Helpers.

See also page 131.

St. Nicholas of Myra

Memorial: December 6

In Byzantine iconography where he is portrayed as the bishop of Myra, St. Nicholas wears a white stole embroidered with crosses draped over his shoulders. The stole, known as an *omophorion* in Greek and a *pallium* in Latin, represents the lost sheep carried on the shoulders of Christ (John 10:1–21). At the same time, the stole symbolizes the bishop's pastoral duties. Traditionally, it was fashioned from lamb's wool, which likely accounts for St. Nicholas's association with spinners. In modern portrayals, however, he is dressed in the vestments worn by a bishop of the Roman Catholic Church.

In Ukraine, St. Nicholas is thought to bring the first snow by shaking his beard. Since he is the patron saint of spinners, yarns and thread were brought to the church on his feast day to add to his beard.

See also pages 80–81, 88–89, 110–11, 114, 121, 133–34, and 182.

St. Petka

Memorial: October 14

Born to noble landowners in the tenth century in the area near modern Istanbul, St. Petka had a profound religious experience at the age of ten that roused her desire to imitate the Lord in his poverty. Over her parents' objections, she began to dress the poor children of her village in her expensive clothes, which were made of the finest spun fabrics. She renounced her family's wealth and ran away to Constantinople, where she lived a devout life of solitude and prayer. The visions she received of the Virgin Mary eventually led her to Jerusalem, where she entered a convent located in the Jordanian desert. A few years later, instructed by an angel, she returned to Constantinople, where she died at the age of twenty-seven. Her relics were translated to Romania in 1641, and her chapel was a site of pilgrimage and healing miracles. Her charitable gifts of fine clothing led to her becoming the patron saint of spinners, weavers, needleworkers, and embroiderers.

St. Seraphina

Memorial: March 12

St. Seraphina of San Gemignano in Tuscany, Italy, was a beautiful, healthy child at her birth in 1238. She was a young saint whose short life was marked by intense suffering. Though her parents were poor, as she grew, she found ways to help those who were even worse off by dividing and sharing her meager meals. She lived the life of a hermit, spinning and sewing during the day and spending her nights in prayer. About the same time her father died, she was stricken with a disease that left her largely paralyzed. She laid on a plank night and day for six years, uniting her pain and suffering to the crucified Christ. St. Seraphina had a special devotion to St. Gregory the Great, who had experienced a similar disease. Eight days before her death on March 12, 1253, St. Gregory appeared to her to tell her that she would obtain her final rest on his feast day. It happened just as he had promised, and when her body was removed from the planks, a bed of white violets was said to have covered the rotted wood. In San Gemignano, the white violets that bloom around the time of her feast day are known to this day as Santa Fina's flowers.

For the Protection of Wool Combers

St. Blaise

Memorial: February 3

St. Blaise was a martyred fourth-century Armenian bishop of Sebastea. He was tortured in 316 by having his flesh torn to bits with sharp iron combs that resembled those used in the preparation of wool for weaving. For this reason, St. Blaise was widely venerated among wool combers during the Middle Ages in areas where the wool trade flourished, including France, Italy, England, Scotland, and Germany. Great celebrations were held, particularly in England, on his feast day. Pageants, live music, and a procession featuring a costumed "St. Blaise" dressed as a bishop, riding on horseback, and carrying a book and a comb, were held.

See also pages 5, 52, 59, and 101.

For the Protection of Cheese Makers

St. Uguzo of Carvagna
Memorial: July 12

St. Uguzo was a poor shepherd who regularly gave all he had to benefit those in greater need. He is credited with having discovered a heat process that increased the cheese yields from milk. Naturally, he gave the resulting surplus cheese to the local poor, to the displeasure of his employer. While the particulars of his life are few, existing accounts report that he was murdered by this employer. Healing water especially beneficial to diseases of the eyes is said to spring from the site where he was killed. St. Uguzo was canonized in the sixteenth century and is depicted in Christian art as a shepherd handing out cheese. He is the patron saint of the elite *Guilde International des Fromagers and Confrérie de Saint-Uguzon.*

Patrons of General Laborers

Farms typically have need of diverse laborers such as carpenters in addition to farmworkers and field hands. In some cases, patron saints of farmworkers serve double duty, but these patron saints are specifically helpful to people who tinker, build, or perform handiwork around the farm.

Bl. Albert of Bergamo
Memorial: May 7 (May 11, Dominicans)

The son of pious peasant farmers, Bl. Albert was born in 1214 in the Lombardy region of northern Italy. As early as the age of seven, he fasted three times a week, giving his portion to the poor. As a married man he was known throughout his hometown for his charity. His wife died at a young age. After her death, Bl. Albert made pilgrimages to Rome, Jerusalem, and Compostela, Spain. His compassion for other pilgrims who fell ill along their journeys led him to build a hospital for their care.

Between his travels, at harvesttime, he worked the fields of Cremona, Italy, with his guardian angel at his side. Accordingly, legend states that his yield of grain was always greater than that of his coworkers, and therefore his wages were twice as much. Out of jealousy, his coworkers planted pieces of iron in the field he worked, expecting that they would dull his scythe and diminish his yield, but his scythe miraculously remained as sharp as ever. He became a Third Order Dominican and, as a lay brother, worked with the Dominican fathers in Cremona to cultivate their herb gardens and perform handiwork around the monastery. Bl. Albert died of natural causes in 1279 in Cremona. Many miracles were attributed to him following his death.

St. James the Greater
Memorial: July 25

Following the death and resurrection of Jesus, St. James shared the gospel in Samaria, Judea, and Spain, where he is said to have preached for nearly forty years. It is believed that Our Lady appeared to him in the year 40, in Saragossa, surrounded by a company of angels (a feat of bilocation, as she was still living) and asked him to build a sanctuary where the Son of God would be honored and glorified. Then she bestowed upon him a pillar of jasper and a statue of her image holding the Christ child to be placed in the sanctuary. At the end of the apparition, she informed St. James that this church would stand until the end of time, and when the sanctuary was completed, he should return to Jerusalem, where his earthly life would come to an end. St. James set to work among many other laborers building the sanctuary, which was the first Christian church ever built. Upon its completion, he returned to Jerusalem. He became, in 44, the first of the apostles to suffer martyrdom. The chapel that St. James constructed, Our Lady of the Pillar, exists today in the form of a magnificent basilica that was erected in the seventeenth century.

See also pages 98 and 102.

St. John Bosco
Memorial: January 31

St. John was born in 1815 in the Piedmont region of Italy. His father passed away when he was just two years old. As he grew older and was able, he took on many odd jobs to help support his family. He learned circus and magic tricks and put on shows, using the entertainment as a draw to share the gospel with the children who watched him perform. Before his ordination in 1841, he worked as a tailor, baker, shoemaker, and carpenter. Upon becoming a priest, he found his greatest joy in teaching and preaching to young people, especially orphans, often rehabilitating the ones who had gone astray. He rented an old barn on a farm and turned it into a home for orphan boys, naming it The Oratory. It became the first of many such homes. He acquired a reputation as a miracle worker when every single one of the boys, whom he mustered as a team to carry local victims of cholera to the hospital or the morgue, were preserved from all sickness and harm. He founded a religious order known as the Salesians of Don Bosco in 1859, whose members dedicated themselves to educating boys under the patronage of Our Lady, Help of Christians, as well as the patronage of St. Francis de Sales. St. John Bosco died in 1888 in Turin, Italy, of natural causes.

St. Joseph the Worker
Memorial: March 19 (St. Joseph) and May 1 (St. Joseph the Worker)

The earthly spouse of Mary, mother of God, and the foster father of Jesus, St. Joseph was, in fulfillment of the Scriptures, a descendant of King David. He was a builder by trade, and while tradition identifies him as a carpenter, other accounts say he was a stoneworker. He was a just and righteous man who demonstrated deep faith in the providential care of God and obedience to his holy will as communicated to him by angels. He cared for and protected the Virgin Mary and the Christ child, taught Jesus the skills of his trade, and is said to have died of natural causes experiencing a happy death in the arms of Jesus and Mary. St. Joseph is often depicted in art holding a lily and a carpenter's square.

In 1955, Pope Pius XII instituted the additional feast of St. Joseph the Worker, which honors St. Joseph as the preeminent model of the holiness of human labor and the dignity of human work. The name of St. Joseph is invoked under this title by persons in need of employment.

See also page 153.
See also page 198 for a Prayer to St. Joseph the Worker.

For the Protection of Mechanics and Wheeled Vehicles

St. Catherine of Alexandria
Memorial: November 25

St. Catherine's association with the torturous breaking wheel led wheelwrights and those who worked with wheeled vehicles and machines to invoke her protection and intercession in times of need. Got tractor, harvester, or automobile troubles? Let St. Catherine of Alexandria hand you the wrench!

See also page 124.

St. Eligius of Noyon

Memorial: December 1

St. Eligius is primarily identified as the patron saint of horses, and thereby also of horse-drawn carriage makers. As technology and transportation progressed, his patronage expanded to include the drivers of taxi cabs and the garages where they were kept. In effect, since taxi cabs kept in garages replaced horse-drawn vehicles kept in stables, St. Eligius naturally assumed the patronage of mechanics who work in modern garages, whether they were located in the city or on a farm.

See also pages 23–24, 44, 99, and 101.

For the Protection of Fruit Dealers

St. Christopher

Memorial: July 25

Legend holds that upon the Christ Child's word, the staff of St. Christopher burst into bloom, specifically, a palm tree bearing fruit, which may explain his connection to fruit dealers. St. Christopher became a missionary preacher of the gospel who, according to St. Ambrose, converted as many as forty-eight thousand souls.

See also pages 104–05 and 182.

For the Protection of Grocers and Farmstand Vendors

St. Amand of Maastricht
Memorial: February 6

Perhaps because of his close association with grapes and his steady diet of bread, St. Amand became the patron saint of grocers. He died at the age of ninety in 676.

See also page 117.

St. Michael the Archangel
Memorial: September 29

One of God's archangels and one of three angels named in the Bible, St. Michael (meaning "Who Is Like God?") led the charge to drive the rebellious angel Lucifer and his minions from heaven, as described in the book of Revelation, chapter 12. He is the supreme guardian and protector of the church against the Antichrist as well as the escort of faithful Christians to heaven at the hour of their death. St. Michael's patronage of grocers may stem from the belief in Eastern churches and iconography that he is the angel who guarded the gate of the Garden of Eden to prevent Adam and Eve from reentering and consuming the fruit of the tree of life. The affinity of grocers with the copious produce of the Garden of Eden—specifically of the tree of life, which bears twelve crops of fruit, yielding its fruit every month (Revelation 22:1–6)—inspires a natural connection to its guardian, St. Michael.

St. Nicholas of Myra
Memorial: December 6

The connection between grocers and St. Nicholas may come from oranges serving as a symbol of the legendary bags of gold St. Nicholas tossed through the windows of impoverished young women in dire need of a proper dowry. It became a tradition to stuff women's stockings with oranges in memory of St. Nicholas's charitable deeds, and grocers may have found this reason enough to invoke his favor in keeping their grocery stores protected and brimming with fresh produce.

See also pages 80–81, 88–89, 110–11, 114, 121, 125, and 182.

For the Protection of Stressed-Out Workers

St. Walter of Pontoise
Memorial: March 23

An esteemed professor of philosophy and rhetoric, when St. Walter of Pontoise tired of worldly pursuits, temptations, and success, he entered a Benedictine abbey in the diocese of Meaux. In 1060, he was recruited by King Philip I to be the first abbot of a new abbey in Pontoise, France. Though he protested, the humble St. Walter had no choice but to accept the position. He struggled, though, leaving his post several times, returning only in obedience to the orders of Pope Gregory VII. He shunned the status of his position, he fought corruption and laziness within the ranks of the clergy, and he suffered imprisonment and beatings at the hands of clergy who resented him. He is said to have spent entire nights in prayer. St. Walter died on Good Friday in 1099. Given his lifetime of hardships on the job, he became known as the patron saint of job-related stress.

For the Protection of Farmers Suffering Financial Hardships

St. Matthew the Apostle
Memorial: September 21

As a first-century Jewish tax collector from Galilee, St. Matthew spent many hours sitting at his booth collecting custom duties from his fellow Jews on behalf of Roman forces. This not only made him extremely unpopular but also branded him a traitor and, in the eyes of the Pharisees, a sinner. All of that changed when Jesus passed by and called him to abandon his post and follow. St. Matthew immediately left his lucrative position to become one of the twelve apostles. He wrote the first Gospel in the New Testament with a Jewish audience in mind, emphasizing Jesus as the Messiah who fulfilled the promises of the Old Testament. He is thought to have died a martyr while evangelizing present-day Egypt.

As the patron saint of accountants, bookkeepers, bankers, and money managers, he is often depicted in art holding a bag of coins or a money box. His close association with finances makes him a saint well acquainted with the complexities of money. It cannot be ignored that he was also a saint who, having left behind everything in order to follow Christ, experienced a life of material poverty.

For the Protection of Early Risers and Oversleepers

St. Vitus
Memorial: June 15

In Rome, St. Vitus cured the possessed son of the Roman emperor Diocletian. Instead of expressing gratitude for the healing, Diocletian charged him with practicing sorcery and demanded that St. Vitus make a sacrifice to his pagan gods. When St. Vitus refused, Diocletian ordered him to be thrown into a pot of boiling oil, into which the emperor also threw a rooster as a sacrificial offering. St. Vitus emerged from the pot unscathed, as though, it is said, from a refreshing bath (the rooster was not so fortunate). He was then ordered to be fed to a lion, which not only refused to harm him but instead crouched before him and licked his feet. He met his end in 303 after being tortured on a rack, and tradition holds that angels came and whisked his body away. A rooster came to be symbolic of St. Vitus; by association, he is invoked for protection against oversleeping and for help in rising early.

See also pages 6 and 18.
See also page 204 for a Deprecatory Blessing against Pests.

For the Protection of Unmarried Farmers' Daughters

St. Coloman of Stockerau
Memorial: October 13

St. Coloman was born the son of an Irish king. As a monk, he set off on pilgrimage to the Holy Land in 1012 by way of the north side of the Danube River. There was a great deal of fighting throughout that region, and his foreign garb and inability to speak German gave rise to accusations that he was a spy. He was arrested and hanged from an elder tree at Stockerau, near Vienna, Austria. No sooner had he been hanged than the tree burst into bloom. His body was left dangling as a warning to enemy forces. Instead, it had the effect of attracting devout locals, who were cured of various ailments simply by touching the corpse, which remained incorrupt with hair and nails that did not stop growing. St. Coloman's body was interred in Melk, which was the Austrian seat of power. The Benedictines founded a shrine there and dedicated it to his honor. By 1089, St. Coloman was adopted as the patron saint of Austria.

It was customary in Austria for unmarried farmers' daughters to pray to St. Coloman for a husband.

———————

Part III

Patron Saints of Places

From apple orchards to vineyards and everywhere in between, there's a patron saint to walk with you, to toil with you, and even to stop and smell the roses with you!

Rumination

Every year just after Thanksgiving, I retrieve cartons of Christmas decorations from the attic and decide which ones will make the cut. Since moving to a farm with a six-stall stable, it's been easier to find places to hang all our lovely reminders of "the reason for the season." Decorating the barn has become a special pleasure, though it requires a little more thought (and height) to keep Pepper, the miniature horse, from making his special brand of mischief.

Just outside the tack room door is a wall of space I've dedicated to horses I have known and loved. On it hang the remnants of a therapeutic shoe worn by my first-ever mare, who suddenly foundered and died. Next to it is a green halter and a peppermint stick, the favorite treat in the world for the gelding I will always remember as the best horse in the world. It's on this memorial wall that I chose to hang a barnwood Christmas sign that says *True love was born in a stable*. Why? Not only because it's a biblical truth but because this stable is also where Dora was born.

Only Kissin' Isadora, a Quarter Horse filly named the feminine form of the patron saint of farmers, St. Isidore, trotted into our hearts on April 29, 2021. Her momma, nineteen-year-old Indy, had landed on our farm two months in foal and in need of groceries and care. The problem was that Indy, who herself had an impressive pedigree, had only known life as a broodmare, due to the break in her withers. She hadn't been handled much. She didn't seem to know or care that she and I were now "in a relationship." She bit me and threatened to kick if I touched her somewhere she didn't like. She definitely did not like men. Fortunately, I had nine more months to win her love and affection. I also had nine more months to figure out this whole business of foaling. Indy was 16.1 hands and too big to safely give birth in our existing stalls. The stable took on a new level of industry as we fashioned a sizeable foaling pen for her in the run-in, and a pass-through to it from her stall. The things we do for love!

Fast forward to the day Indy showed signs of going into labor. I'd heard that most mares give birth in the wee hours of the night and prepared myself to camp out in the barn. I had an image of St. Anne, a patron saint for the protection of stables and the patron saint of grandmothers (even nervous grandmothers of foals, I reasoned!) posted on the wall. Bless her heart, as they say in the South. Indy must have known I was a rookie, since she kindly gave birth at four o'clock in the afternoon.

We didn't miss a minute of it. Isadora's arrival was miraculous and flawless and uncomplicated, and accompanied by the kind of awe reserved for those first breathtaking and breath-giving moments of new life. The bond between mare and foal was instant. Yes, there were maternal instincts in play. But I know firsthand that horses love. They love their babies. They love each other. And they love me (even Indy!). Dora added more love to the stable the day she was born. It was already a sacred space, sanctified by our love and prayers, by blessed salt and holy water, and chiefly by the presence of God and his holy angels and saints. Over the course of the next several months, more and more people would fall in love with Dora. The miracle of her life, which came into its fullness of being in our stable, has inspired so much joy and wonder. Even our equine vet fell for Dora, so much so that he purchased her. Indeed, true love was born in a stable in so many wonderful ways!

Wherever there is life—in stables, orchards, gardens, vineyards, crop fields, flower beds, barns, or the family farmhouse—the love that is sown is the love that is grown and multiplies for the life of the world.

Praise be the Child who was born in a stable and who in every place and season is LORD of all!

For the Protection of Apple Orchards

St. Charles Borromeo
Memorial: November 4

Born to nobility in 1538 in the castle of Arona just outside Milan, Italy, St. Charles showed great sanctity from his youth. His pious family recognized the inevitability of his vocation to religious life, and at the age of twelve he was sent to live and study at a Benedictine abbey in Arona. Thereafter, he enrolled in a university in Pavia, where he studied civil and canon law, despite a speech impediment that made him appear slow, graduating in 1559 with a degree in law. He returned to Milan, where his uncle, Pope Pius IV, had just been elected pope. St. Charles advanced both in holiness and in ecclesiastical office, which culminated in his appointment as the archbishop and cardinal of Milan. In this capacity, St. Charles was a champion of sweeping reforms throughout the church. During the plague that struck Milan in 1576, his quiet service ministering to the sick and burying the dead endeared him to the people of Milan. He also founded seminaries, hospitals, and schools, and survived an attempt on his life. He died in 1584 from a fever.

Due to severe (some say intestinal) sickness that struck him in his twenties, St. Charles was extreme in his diet and penitential practices, which included living almost entirely on bread and water, to which, on Sundays and holy days, he occasionally added an apple. During Lent, he ate only dried figs and boiled beans. He was likely declared a patron saint of apple orchards because apples were his sole indulgence and because his feast day occurs during the fall harvesting of apples.

St. Kevin of Glendalough
Memorial: June 3

One of the legends of St. Kevin involves a poor young man with epilepsy who lived near the monastery. Having received divine word that he would be cured by eating an apple from the monastery, this young man set out to beg the monks at the monastery for an apple. St. Kevin happened to be the monk who greeted him. St. Kevin listened with compassion. The problem was that there was not one single apple tree in their fields. Nevertheless, St. Kevin went into action. He blessed a grove of willow trees and then commanded them to bear fruit—specifically, apples—and they did. The young man ate the miraculous fruit and was healed. The willows continued to produce "St. Kevin's apples," which were distributed throughout Ireland for the next four centuries.

See also pages 33–34, 64, and 65.

See also page 207 for the Blessing of Orchards and Vineyards.

———

Patrons of Planting and Crop Fields

Some saints are invoked for the general protection of the fields,
while others are invoked at the time of seeding or harvesting.
Farmers need look no further than this "crop" of saints for
abundant help and blessings.

For the Protection of the Harvesting of Planting and Crop Fields

St. Agnes of Rome
Memorial: January 21

In Lithuania and other Eastern European countries, St. Agnes's feast day (which was celebrated for many years on January 28) corresponded to pagan celebrations on the first few days of February to honor Gabija, the goddess of fire, corn, and other grains. The combination of fire with grains had led people to accord bread as a gift emanating from Gabija's influence. With the rise of Christianity, the celebration of the feast day of St. Agnes took precedence over pagan celebrations, and the bread once attributed to the goddess became known as St. Agnes's Bread. On her feast day, bread, water, and salt are consecrated by the local priest and then divided among family members to consume and to distribute wherever the need existed. In Lithuania, for instance, it became the custom for plowmen who were venturing out for the first plowing of the season to tie a piece of St. Agnes's bread to the plow shaft in the prayerful hope that this would prevent the sun from burning the crops. In eastern and southeastern Lithuania, when farmers were sowing flax seed, it was traditional to tie St. Agnes's bread to the seeder so that the new flax fibers would grow to be very white.

See also pages 103–104.

St. Ansovinus of Camerino
Feast Day: March 13

A native of Camerino, Italy, and pious from his youth, St. Ansovinus became a priest and then the bishop of Camerino in the mid-ninth century. He was best known for his concern for the poor. Once, when the granary was depleted, he prayed for the means to feed hungry people seeking help, and the granary was miraculously replenished. He was known during his lifetime and after his death both for performing healing miracles as well as for relieving famine. His miracle of the granary most likely led farmers to adopt St. Ansovinus as a patron and protector of their grain fields.

St. Anthony of Padua
Memorial: June 13

A field of wheat which was the sole source of an elderly woman's sustenance was being ravaged by flocks of sparrows. She promised St. Anthony that she would pray at his tomb nine times in exchange for his blessing and the restoration of her field. Confident in his intercession, she did not check on the field until she had completed her novena. When she returned, there was not a sparrow to been seen. That year, she reaped a more bountiful harvest than ever before.

Following St. Francis's death, St. Anthony returned to Italy by way of La Provence, where he and his companions took rest at a poor widow's house. The widow nourished them with baked bread and wine. In her haste, she neglected to turn off the tap to the wine barrel and the barrel ran dry. To make matters worse, one of St. Anthony's companions broke his wine glass. The good saint prayed. Miraculously, the glass was made whole, and the wine barrel refilled to the brim with wine. Perhaps this is what makes St. Anthony the ultimate patron saint of "bread and wine"!

See also pages 27–28, 53, and 58.
See also page 197 for the Prayer of St. Anthony.
See also page 203 for the Prayer to St. Anthony for Lost Animals.

The Blessed Virgin Mary
Memorial: August 15 (Feast of the Assumption)

Dating back to the Middle Ages, the Feast of the Assumption memorializes the earthly end of the life of Mary, the mother of God, when Mary was assumed into heaven. Tradition calls for farmers to bless and dedicate to God the first fruits, grains, and herbs of their harvest, many of which ripen in mid-August. The blessing of herbs is particular to the Feast of the Assumption, and traditionally included flowers both wild and cultivated, as well as healing herbs, which were blessed by being placed upon or underneath the altar cloth, where they would be privileged with close contact with the Eucharist. The institution of this blessing on the Feast Day of the Assumption corresponds to the tradition stemming from three days after her death, when her tomb was opened by the apostles to satisfy the late arrival of St. Thomas, who wished to venerate her body. Astonishingly, in the place where the body of the Virgin should have been, the tomb was overflowing with lilies and roses. Thus it was understood that the mother of God had been assumed, body and soul, straight up into heaven.

See also pages 123–24 and 149–50.
See also pages 222–24 for a Blessing of Herbs.

St. Engelmaro
Memorial: January 14

Born into poverty in Bavaria, Germany, in the early twelfth century, St. Engelmaro was a peasant laborer who became a hermit in a forest near Passau, Germany. Until his death, the pious Armenian hermit named Gregory, a former bishop who had retired to the forest to die, was St. Engelmaro's sole companion. Following the death of his friend, St. Engelmaro tried to remain in solitude, but the people of nearby Windberg, knowing him to be both wise and holy, flocked to him for advice.

He was murdered on January 13, 1100, by a local man who was both envious of St. Engelmaro's popularity and convinced that the saint was in possession of a store of treasure. St. Engelmaro's body was concealed in a snow drift until a spring thaw. A dazzling display of light led people to discover where it had lain. This event has been reenacted through the years in a local custom called "searching for Engelmaro." According to this tradition, an image of St. Engelmaro is hidden in the forest. After it is found, it is carried by solemn procession to the church where his relics reside. St. Englemaro's association with the harvest relates to the time of year—after the spring thaw, when the fields were tilled to prepare for the planting of new crops—when his body was found.

St. Florian of Lorch
Memorial: May 4

St. Florian was a high-ranking officer in the third-century Roman army. However, he had secretly converted to Christianity. Two different accounts of actions leading to his martyrdom survive. One holds that he refused to offer sacrifice to Roman gods, the other that he defied orders to execute a group of Christians. In either case, he was martyred for his bold profession. He was scourged, flayed, and set on fire and, in a final barbaric punishment, he was thrown into the River Ems near Lorch with a millstone tied around his neck, there to drown. An eagle spread its wings over his body, which enabled it to be found and retrieved by a woman of faith who brought it to an Augustinian abbey.

In Poland, where he is the country's patron saint, devotion to St. Florian first assimilated with, then gradually replaced, the homage paid to Pergrubrius, the Baltic god of flowers, plants, and all things agricultural. Polish folklore states, *If on St. Florian's day the rain is torrential, the harvest will be abundant, good, and clean.*

See also pages 179 and 183.

St. Gregory of Ostia
Memorial: May 9

St. Gregory was a Benedictine monk and priest who resided in Rome, Italy, at the monastery of Sts. Cosmas and Damian. Around 1034, he was chosen to be the bishop, then cardinal, of Ostia, Italy. He died in 1048 while serving as papal legate to the kingdoms of Navarre and Old Castille, in Spain. St.

Gregory was known as a miracle worker whose specialty was saving crops from pests, especially locusts. He is said to have freed the kingdom of Navarre from a devastating plague of locusts, repelling them by leading people in prayer and then making the sign of the cross over the fields.

St. John the Apostle
Memorial: December 27

St. John the Apostle's connection with the harvest is reflected in his Gospel accounts, when, for example, Jesus says, "Amen, amen, I say to you, unless a grain of wheat falls to the ground and dies, it remains just a grain of wheat; but if it dies, it produces much fruit" (John 12:24). Similarly, in the book of Revelation, St. John records in dramatic detail the great harvest of the earth which is meant to represent the gathering of the elect at the Apocalypse. Farmers may have taken special note of these agriculture references. Moreover, St. John was and continues to be an extraordinary harvester of souls for Christ through his deeds and by means of his writings.

See also pages 87, 119, and 186.

St. Medard of Noyon
Memorial: June 8

The son of fifth-century nobles and a brother to the bishop of Rouen, France, St. Medard showed signs of a religious vocation from his youth, when he often traveled on business with his father throughout France and Belgium. Following his studies, he was ordained and became the bishop of Vermand, and later of Noyon, France, and Tournai, Belgium. According to legend, as a child he was sheltered from rain by an eagle, which led to his association as a weather saint and as a patron of those who work in the fields. Harvesters looked to this saint's feast day to predict the weather during the growing season: *If it rains on his feast day, the next forty days will be wet. If the weather is dry, the next forty days will be so also.* St. Medard died in 545 of natural causes.

Patrons of Gardens and Flower Gardens

*While any of the patron saints of gardeners can be embraced as
a patron saint of gardens, the queen of the garden is the rose,
and the Queen of Heaven and earth and all the saints is the
Blessed Virgin Mary, mother of God. As the patroness of all
humanity and therefore of all human activity, Our Lady's
association with gardening, gardens, and cultivating flowers of
all kinds is a time-honored tradition.*

St. Elizabeth of Hungary
Memorial: November 17

The daughter of a Hungarian king, St. Elizabeth was married to Prince Louis of Thuringia at the age of thirteen. She demonstrated great concern for the poor and the sick, building a hospital at the foot of the mountain upon which her castle was perched. She cited Christ's teachings as her motivation in all things, including the feeding of the poor. Against her husband's wishes, she often took bread from their household to share with the needy. It is said that when her husband questioned what was inside her apron, the loaves of bread she was hiding miraculously turned into roses. As the patron saint of rose gardens, she is often depicted wearing a crown of roses and carrying bread. St. Elizabeth died in 1231 of natural causes.

St. Mary, Mother of God
Memorial: January 1

From the earliest of times, the rose has been a symbol of Mary. During the Middle Ages, the rose was cultivated in monastery gardens for its primacy of beauty and medicinal value. St. Ambrose held that beds of thornless roses had bloomed in the Garden of Eden, sprouting thorns only after the advent of original sin. Mary, having been conceived without sin, is therefore known as the Rose without Thorns. The story of Our Lady of Guadalupe and the miraculous presence of roses in winter (1591) epitomizes Mary's association with roses. According to St. Cardinal Newman, Mary is known as the Mystical Rose not only because she is the Queen of spiritual flowers but also because she is hidden (or mystical). The rosary, originally called the Psalter of Mary, is itself a symbol of a garland of roses.

Though her connection to roses is particularly strong, Mary also has an association with flowers of all kinds. There was a time when almost every plant that blossomed was given a common Marian name that symbolized an aspect of her holy life or character. Flowers closely connected to Mary include the lily (as a symbol of innocence and virginity), the iris (also known as the sword lily, symbolizing her sorrow), the periwinkle (whose blue color echoes the blue of Mary's robes), and the marigold (as a reference to her heavenly glory). Columbine, also known as Our Lady's Shoes because the dropped petals resemble a slipper, is said to have sprung from the ground wherever Mary stepped as she famously made her way to visit her cousin Elizabeth.

St. Mary Garden, which is the earliest known garden devoted exclusively to Mary, was cultivated in France in the seventh century by the patron saint of gardeners, St. Fiacre. The garden surrounded an oratory and hospice that St. Fiacre built and dedicated to Mary.

See also pages 123–24 and 145.

For the Protection of Organic Gardens and Farms

St. Patrick
Memorial: March 17

St. Patrick is well known for having used the shamrock to illustrate the doctrine of the Holy Trinity as he introduced Christianity to Ireland. However, the symbol of the shamrock progressed to become a nineteenth-century symbol of political rebellion, and anyone wearing it risked death by hanging. This period of uprising gave birth to the phrase "the wearin' o' the green." In modern times, "green" has become the catchword for all things eco-friendly. Thus has St. Patrick become an adopted patron saint of the organic farming and gardening movements.

See also pages 16–17.

For the Protection of Vineyards

St. Gratus of Aosta
Memorial: September 7
Among his many miracles, St. Gratus, a fifth-century Italian bishop of Aosta, Italy, is said to have thwarted a plague of grasshoppers. Later, in the 1400s, his name was invoked against a plague of insects in the Tarentaise region of France. A threefold blessing ceremony of the earth, water, and candles attached to St. Gratus coincides with the beginning of spring. He died of natural causes around 470 in Aosta.

Wine growers in the Valle d'Aosta, which today produce what is known as Alpine wines, call upon St. Gratus for protection against insect damage. In addition, they ask his intercession to shield their delicate vineyards. In art, St. Gratus is depicted as a bishop carrying a bunch of grapes and the head of St. John the Baptist, which he is said to have unearthed because of a dream.

See also pages 12 and 171.

St. Severinus of Noricum
Memorial: January 8
Born in 410 to a family of Roman nobles in North Africa, St. Severinus renounced his inheritance and abandoned his homeland to become a hermit in the Egyptian desert. In response to a call to evangelize, he left his eremitical life to preach and teach in Noricum, now in modern Austria. He founded centers of refuge for those who had been rendered homeless by the invasion of

the Huns. He established monasteries to revitalize the region. His prayers once dispersed a swarm of locusts that threatened to destroy a harvest. He settled somewhere outside Vienna at a location recorded as "at the vineyards" but subsequently returned to Vienna, taking up residence in a cell on a hillside, where he was joined by his disciples. St. Severinus is said to have died in 482 while singing Psalm 150. His relics were translated to Naples, Italy, six years after his death, where they reside in a church that bears his name.

For the Protection of Rural Communities

St. Isidore the Farmer
Memorial: May 15
St. Isidore was proclaimed the patron saint of farmers at the 1947 United States' National Catholic Rural Conference. Catholic Rural Life is a nonprofit organization that has promoted Catholic life in rural America for nearly 100 years.

See also pages 31, 62, 79, and 165.
See also page 197 for a Prayer Invoking St. Isidore the Farmer.
See also page 218 for the Blessing of a Well.

For the Protection of Stables and Barns

St. Guy of Anderlecht
Memorial: September 12
St. Guy is associated predominantly with horses, and therefore with the stables in which they are kept. His intercession is sought for the protection of all kinds of stables, including modern-day horse barns and shed rows.

See also pages 32 and 46.
See also page 212 for a Blessing of a Stable.

For the Protection of Domestic Homes and Farmhouses

St. Joseph
Memorial: March 19

As the patron saint of the universal church, St. Joseph's paternal protection also extends to the home and to family life, which can be thought of as the domestic church. Because the spiritual life of the family grows within the walls of our homes and upon the land where we dwell, both are necessarily ennobled as sacred spaces where God is honored and prayers are prayed. St. Joseph protects all of these living spaces as his own.

See also page 131.
See also page 211 for a Blessing of a Home or Farmhouse.

———

Part IV

Patron Saints of Weather and Protectors against Natural Disasters

In 326, three crosses were discovered in Jerusalem deep in the earth at a place St. Helen had excavated in her quest to discover the True Cross of Christ's crucifixion. The inscribed sign ordered by Pilate mocking Jesus as the King of the Jews, though no longer attached to a cross, was also excavated from the pit at the foot of Calvary, along with the nails and the crown of thorns. So as to make no mistake identifying which of the three crosses had borne the body of Christ, Macarius, the bishop of Jerusalem, prayed, and then had a dying woman who suffered from a "dangerous malady" touch each cross with her hand. The first two crosses produced no effect. Upon touching the third cross, however, the woman was miraculously healed, thereby revealing the True Cross. The day of the finding of the Holy Cross was recorded as May 3, which is why on this day crosses are blessed and set in fields, vineyards, gardens, and farms in celebration of the victory of the cross as the faithful seek divine protection against adverse weather.

Rumination

Tornado season. The very thought of it struck fear into my heart when my husband and I moved to Middle Tennessee, to a small town in a large track known as Dixie Alley. The limestone bedrock common to our area makes homes with basements scarce. That's why we had bolted a four-by-six-by seven-foot welded steel box to our garage floor, a family-safe shelter engineered to withstand an F5 tornado. Theoretically, if such a weather event occurred, we'd huddle inside until the tornado passed and emerge from our armored cocoon to squint into what remained. Since then, we've had more than one occasion to test that theory. Despite reassurances by the locals that a tornado hadn't touched down in "these parts" for ages, just three weeks after moving in, we were jolted out of bed by a screaming weather radio, warning us that a tornado was on the ground nearby.

Okay. Grab the dog. Grab my phone. Grab the car keys and, oh yeah, grab my husband! My heart pounds and adrenaline surges. This is no dress rehearsal. While I'd known before bedtime that severe overnight thunderstorms were possible—the kind that spawn tornadoes—I had kept reminding myself: *not in these parts . . . not in these parts*!

I swing open the heavy door to our shelter as a throaty rumble of thunder steals my last ounce of courage. Our golden retriever is goofing off and thinks this is a game. My groggy husband moves like blackstrap molasses and wants to go back to bed. I'm testy and frightened and despite the fact that I can barely breathe, I'm in hypercontrol and barking orders on how to batten the hatches. In that moment, I think there are not enough angels and saints in the world to save us from ourselves.

And then, I remember.

I remember St. Barbara, a patron saint against severe storms, who was confined by her cruel father for years in a cramped room at the top of a high tower. Surely, she knows what it feels like to be crouched in a corner, clutching rosary beads and praying for deliverance. I remember St. Scholastica, a patron saint against thunderstorms, who used to meet her beloved brother, St. Benedict, once a year at a farmstead located halfway between his monastery and her convent. Surely, she recalls the joys of hearth, home, and family that she found in a cozy farmhouse, and will hasten to defend ours. I remember St. Thomas Aquinas, whose younger sister was killed by lightning while sleeping in the same room as him when he himself was just a child, and who as a traumatized adult would duck into a church to pray at the first sign of a storm. Surely, he experienced the gut-twisting terror that brings me to my knees. In the darkness, I invoke all three saints for serenity and security, along with St. Eligius of Noyon, to whom I entrust our horses in the barn. Swiftly, the peace of Christ enters this cold steel vault and transforms it into a sacred space. The storm rages on but my fear subsides. I have a supernatural confidence that all shall be well.

Twenty minutes later, it is.

In reading the following pages, may you, too, come to know and remember these saints in waiting who are eager to help in every kind of weather. Find the ones who speak to your heart and your needs, and trust in their friendship and intercession—come rain or come shine!

For Protection against Cold Weather

St. Maurus
Memorial: January 15 (before 1969), November 22 (after 1969)

Born in 512 in Rome, Italy, to a noble family, St. Maurus began his studies as a disciple of St. Benedict at the age of twelve. He became a Benedictine monk, and served as an assistant to St. Benedict in both Subiaco and Monte Cassino, in Italy. In 542 he founded an abbey in France. His reputation for healing miracles grew. These included bringing the dead back to life through a combination of prayers and blessing the afflicted with a relic of the True Cross. He died in 584 of natural causes. Unfortunately, his relics, which were interred inside a church in Paris, were destroyed during the French Revolution.

Legend has it that one day at the monastery in Subiaco, St. Benedict had a vision of a young monk being swept away in the river while he was fetching water. Immediately, he dispatched St. Maurus to the riverbank to rescue their fellow monk. In blind obedience to his Superior, St. Maurus immediately rushed to the riverbank, where he saved the monk from drowning by walking across the water to get to the young man. Later, St. Maurus refused to accept praise for having played any part in the miraculous rescue, preferring instead to give credit to the intercession of St. Benedict.

Those who suffer from the cold, as well as those seeking protection from it, find help and solace in this most humble, obedient saint.

St. Sebaldus
Memorial: August 19

An eighth-century missionary saint who was likely raised in England, St. Sebaldus forsook his noble birth for an eremitic life. He traveled throughout Germany, preaching, evangelizing, and working miracles among nonbelievers. In addition to converting stones to bread in order to feed his brother missionaries, during the winter he used icicles as firewood to warm the local poor and keep them from freezing to death.

It is said that during a particularly brutal cold spell when he was living as a hermit, he sought shelter and a warm fire at a nearby home. The miserly owner refused. The saint asked his wife to pray for her husband's change of heart, which she did, to no avail. Turning to Plan B, the saint asked the man's wife to go outside and gather icicles. After he prayed over them, the icicles ignited in the hearth as if they were kindling wood. Seeing this, the husband repented and praised God for the miracle.

St. Sebaldus died in 770. He was buried at the place in Nuremburg where the oxen carting his body stopped and refused to travel further.

For Protection against Frost

St. Sophia of Rome
Memorial: May 15

St. Sophia was a pious second-century Christian widow who lived in Italy. Her three daughters were christened after the virtues of Faith, Hope, and Love, and were raised by their mother to boldly proclaim the gospel. An official of the Roman emperor Hadrian had the four women arrested and brought to Rome, where each of the girls, in turn, suffered various tortures right before their mother's eyes. None of them recanted their faith or made a sacrifice to the goddess Artemis. After enduring great suffering, the girls were beheaded. St. Sophia was permitted the privilege of burying their bodies. The three coffins were drawn by wagon to a hill outside the city, where they were buried. St. Sophia kept vigil beside the graves for three days before dying herself.

Though she herself did not suffer physical torture, the deep suffering she experienced in her heart earned her status as a martyr. St. Sophia's name is invoked against late frosts and for the protection of crops perhaps because her feast day marks the last day of cold weather in parts of Central Europe. For this reason, she is known as one of the Ice Saints. In Germany, she is also known as Cold Sophia by those who seek her aid in planting frost-free crops.

St. Urban of Langres
Memorial: April 2

Frost on delicate, young grapevine shoots is a serious, potentially devastating springtime threat. The timing of St. Urban's feast day combined with his close connection to vintners and vineyards makes him a powerful intercessor and protector against the loss of any crop due to frost. In Germany, local folklore is expressed in the adage, *Sunshine on St. Urban's Day, the wine thrives afterward, they say.*

See also page 117.

For Rain and for Protection against Drought

St. Agricola of Avignon
Memorial: September 2

Born in 625 in France to a widowed father who became a monk and then the bishop of Avignon, at the age of sixteen, St. Agricola also became a monk, in Lérins, France. In time, he was ordained. In 660, he was named co-bishop of Avignon, where he built a Benedictine convent and became known for his charity and staunch defense of the poor and marginalized. It is said that his prayers produced rain and heralded good weather. He died around the year 700 of natural causes. By virtue of his name, which translates to "cultivator of fields," as well as the good and holy works he accomplished in his lifetime, it was "right as rain" for the farming community of Avignon to seek his intercession for good weather, and for rain during times of drought.

St. Angadrisma of Beauvais
Memorial: October 14

Invoked particularly against drought, St. Angadrisma was born in France in the seventh century. From an early age, she took a vow of virginity. Unaware of her vow, her noble parents promised her in marriage to St. Ansbert of Chaussy.

When St. Angadrisma prayed for a miracle to thwart the marriage so that she could pursue a religious vocation, she was immediately stricken with leprosy. She rejoiced at the affliction, believing it to be a saving grace sent from her beloved, Jesus Christ. Her marriage was called off, her betrothed married another, and St. Angadrisma became a nun. As soon as she took the veil, her leprosy was miraculously healed.

Having become a Benedictine abbess in a monastery near Beauvais, she once stopped a raging fire by holding up a relic of the monastery's founder, St. Ebrulf of Ouche. Because the flames were immediately extinguished, her patronage against searing heat and the parching effects of drought was firmly established.

St. Cataldus of Taranto
Memorial: May 10

St. Cataldus was said as a newborn infant to have brought his deceased mother back to life when his tiny fingers brushed against her corpse. He presented many signs of sanctity from a young age, and grew up to become the headmaster of a monastic school in Lismore, Ireland. He became a priest and a worker of miracles.

A silver statue of St. Cataldus clad in pontifical vestments and holding his left hand out as though to impart a blessing receives special veneration in Taranto, Italy, where he had served the locals as a beloved bishop. The statue is washed clean on feast days, and the water that runs over it is collected and distributed to the faithful as a source of miraculous cures. When droughts threatened to destroy the vineyards and crops of Calabria, the statue was carried over the parched lands, and rain was said to fall soon afterward. Though he always longed to return to his beloved Ireland, St. Cataldus died of natural causes around 685 in Taranto.

See also page 169.

St. Comasia
Memorial: November 5

St. Comasia is a third-century Roman martyr about whom little is known. Her remains were discovered in the catacombs of St. Agnes in Rome. In the mid-1600s, her relics were translated by papal decree to a shrine in Martina Franca, Italy, beneath a long, steady rain that seemed to follow their delivery to the city. The area of Martina Franca is steeped in agriculture, and the urn that holds St. Comasia's relics is carried in procession over the land as protection against drought conditions.

St. Eulalia of Barcelona
Memorial: February 12

As a brave and pious thirteen-year-old virgin martyr in a Christian family, St. Eulalia resisted her mother's efforts to escape to the remote countryside to avoid the persecutions of the Roman emperor Diocletian. Instead, in 304, the young teen marched into the town's court where she boldly professed her faith and protested the emperor's treatment of Christians. The amused Roman judge gave her a chance to recant her faith and worship his pagan gods, but when she refused, he became enraged. He then subjected her to a series of thirteen tortures, one for every year of her life. At last, she was crucified. At her death it began to snow. As the snowflakes covered her naked body, a white dove flew from her mouth.

According to legend, a drought had struck the area of Barcelona (then called Barcino) when St. Eulalia was a young child. She had gone to draw water from a nearby well, only to find that it had run dry. She put her shawl over the well, and water began to flow so copiously that it changed into a river. She was canonized in 633 and declared a patron saint of Barcelona. However, things changed when, in 1687, Barcelona was struck with a terrible plague of locusts. People prayed to Our Lady of Mercy for deliverance. When the plague ended, the people continued to seek the intercession of Our Lady of Mercy over the child martyr. It is said that whenever it rains on the Feast of Our Lady of Mercy, the raindrops are the tears of St. Eulalia, who is no longer frequently called upon for help.

St. Godeberta of Noyon
Memorial: April 11

Born in the seventh century to a noble family near Amiens, France, St. Godeberta was encouraged to become a nun by St. Eligius, who was then the bishop of Noyon. Inspired by the Holy Spirit, she dedicated her life to God by entering a convent, eventually serving as abbess. It is said that when Noyon was engulfed by a raging fire, St. Godeberta had only to make the sign of the cross over the flames and they were miraculously extinguished. Her interces- sion is said to similarly protect against the searing effects of drought. She died around 700 in Noyon of natural causes.

St. Heribert of Cologne
Memorial: March 16

St. Heribert, the son of Duke Hugo of Worms, in Germany, was born in the tenth century. In 994, after receiving an elite education, he was ordained to the priesthood. In 999, he was named the archbishop of Cologne. He was widely regarded for his piety, charity to the poor, the founding of a Benedictine monastery, and the founding of the church of Deutz. He is often depicted in art as an archbishop praying for rain. It is said that amid a drought, St. Heribert led a prayer procession from St. Severin to St. Pantaleon in Cologne, during which a dove was seen circling above his head. Following the Mass that was celebrated at the end of the procession, the rain came pouring down.

St. Honoratus of Arles
Memorial: January 16

Born in 350 in northern Gaul and having converted to Christianity as a young man, St. Honoratus lived as a monk in Greece, Egypt, and Palestine. Upon his return to his homeland, he founded the Abbey of Lérins on a small island off the coastline of France. In 426, he became the archbishop of Arles, Gaul, and was beloved and revered by the people of Arles. When he died in 429 of natural causes, they flocked to his tomb, snatching pieces of his funeral shroud as holy relics.

It is said when St. Honoratus arrived at Lérins, the island was infested with serpents, which St. Honoratus was fearless in banishing. He also caused springs of sweet water to flow throughout the previously dry, barren land, which gave rise to his patronage of people praying for rain.

St. Isidore the Farmer
Memorial: May 15

It is said that when St. Isidore's toddler-aged son fell into a deep well, St. Isidore prayed for divine assistance, and the well water miraculously rose up to ground level, thus saving the little boy from drowning. To further solidify St. Isidore's association with water and rain, more than once during the thirteenth century and beyond, St. Isidore's incorrupt body was extracted from his tomb to be placed before the altar of St. Andrew's Church, where the faithful kept vigil as they prayed through the merits of this saint for abundant rainfall to end the drought that threatened everyone with famine. St. Isidore never failed to intercede. Every time, rains fell upon the parched land.

See also pages 31, 62, 79, and 152.
See also page 197 for a Prayer Invoking St. Isidore the Farmer.
See also page 218 for the Blessing of a Well.

St. Modan
Memorial: February 4

St. Modan was born in Ireland but lived the greater part of his life in Scotland. As a monk, he prayed eight hours every day. While he preferred to be just another humble monk at the Dryburgh Abbey in Melrose, Scotland, eventually he was appointed its abbot. He retired after many years, whereupon he chose complete solitude in Dumbarton, Scotland. During times of drought, he was called out of retirement to create a spring of water by planting his staff into the ground. The miraculous appearance of the spring was his cue to return to the solitude of his cell. He died in the sixth century in Dumbarton of natural causes.

St. Odo of Cluny
Memorial: November 18

Born in France around 879, St. Odo's noble parents provided him a prestigious Parisian education in music and theology. He returned home four years later, but confined himself to a hermit's cell, where he continued to study and pray in the Benedictine tradition. He became a monk, priest, abbot, and founder of monasteries in France and Italy, and was known as a reformer, peacemaker, writer, composer, and helper of the poor. Throughout his life, he fostered an intense devotion to St. Martin, to whom he had been consecrated at birth and to whom he attributed his miraculous cure from a sickness that struck him when he was sixteen. He died in 942 of natural causes.

During his reforms, St. Odo enforced the *Rule of St. Benedict* against the eating of meat, allowing only fish to be consumed. He visited St. Elias's monastery in Nepi, Italy, and when he discovered that there was a scarcity of fish, he caused a stream teaming with fish to miraculously flow from a nearby mountain. His influence over water was also highlighted when fellow monks rescued a precious old book on the life of St. Martin from rising floodwaters. The book had been left in the monastery's cellar, where St. Odo had been working on creating a glossary for the volume. Despite having weathered the torrential rainstorm, the margins of the book were soaked but the text was dry. They marveled at the miracle, which they attributed to St. Odo's additions to the book. St. Odo, however, gave the glory to God and to his patron.

St. Solange
Memorial: May 10

St. Solange was a virgin shepherdess known for her profound love of animals and for the power to heal them. Born in 863, she was martyred at the age of seventeen by one of the sons of the count of Poitier.

Legend holds that upon her beheading, St. Solange's mouth thrice invoked the name of Jesus, then she picked up her severed head and walked with it to the church of St. Martin in a village that now bears her name. There, she finally died. Devotion to her as a miracle worker quickly spread. The local church where her head was preserved as a relic assumed her name in 1281, and a nearby field where she was known to pray was named for her. In times of drought in the seventeenth century, locals processed through Bourges accompanied by the head of St. Solange, confident that their beloved saint would bring forth rain.

See also page 96.
See also page 215 for a Prayer for Rain.

St. Swithun
Memorial: July 15

Born at the turn of the ninth century in England, St. Swithun was a monk, priest, preacher, tutor, and counselor to royalty. Ultimately, he served as the bishop of Winchester, England. During his lifetime, he rebuilt decaying churches, performed miracles, and set an example for his flock of true humility and devotion to God. As often as he was able, he invited the local poor to festive banquets rather than wealthy, fashionable citizens. On his deathbed, he asked to be buried outside the Cathedral at Winchester because it was a place where "passersby might tread on his grave and where the rain from the eaves might fall on it." Following his death in 862, his devotees, who attributed many miracles over the next one hundred years to the veneration of his relics, attempted to move his remains from this earthen grave to a more elaborate shrine inside the cathedral. The deceased saint demonstrated his disapproval of the plan with a rainfall that continued for forty days. According to folklore, on the July 15 anniversary of the transfer of his relics, the adage goes that *On St. Swithun's Day, if thou dost rain, for forty days it will remain. St. Swithun's Day, if thou be fair, for forty days 'twill rain nae mair.*

St. Trophimus of Arles
Memorial: December 29

St. Trophimus was a confessor saint and bishop of Arles, in Gaul, now modern France, in the mid-third century. St. Gregory of Tours himself was an admirer, saying of St. Trophimus that he lived his life "in great holiness, winning many people over to the church." On a side note, some sources hold that he is the same first-century Trophimus mentioned in the book of Acts who was sent as a missionary to Gaul by St. Paul.

The relics of St. Trophimus were transferred from the cemetery of the Church of St. Honoratus on the outskirts of Arles to a cathedral that, in the tenth century, was under the patronage of St. Stephen, after which this church was dedicated to St. Trophimus. In 1152, his relics were permanently moved to the newly built cathedral in Arles that bears his name. Geographically, Arles is perched on an elevated platform of limestone rock, and was reputed to be the sole dry spot for miles around. As a result, particularly on a nearby plateau called the Elysian Fields (Alyscans), it became highly valued as a dry resting place for the dead. This quality of aridness may have given rise to St. Trophimus's intercession in bringing rain to the dusty, dry land. If one were to adhere to the tradition that St. Trophimus was a traveling companion of St. Paul, then one would also believe that he, along with St. Paul, was beheaded under the command of the Roman emperor Nero.

For Protection against Storms and Lightning

St. Agrippina of Rome
Memorial: June 23

Born in the third century to a noble Roman family, St. Agrippina, said to be a beautiful, fair-haired princess, was martyred for the faith in 256 by the Roman emperor Valerian, whose romantic advances she may have spurned. Her relics were moved from Rome to Mineo, Sicily, by her sisters, Bassa, Paula, and Agathonice. Tradition states that these sisters were able to single-handedly transport the heavy reliquary because miraculously it was made light for the journey. It is said that dense, dark clouds offered them protective cover during the most dangerous moments of their sacred mission. The three women and St. Agrippina's relics arrived safely in Mineo on May 14, 261.

St. Barbara
Memorial: December 4

St. Barbara was a third-century virgin martyr who was born in Nicomedia, in ancient Greece. Because of her beauty, and wanting to protect her from insults, her pagan father confined St. Barbara to a high tower, where she received instruction in the arts, philosophy, and literature by visiting tutors. Exposure to new thoughts led her to reject polytheism and convert to Christianity. Enraged by his daughter's conversion, and at the command of the local authorities, her father set out to kill her. She escaped, but was caught, fiercely tortured, and beheaded by her own father. Immediately, in an act of divine retribution, her father was struck dead by lightning (by some accounts, fire from heaven). Not surprisingly, then, she is invoked for safekeeping against severe storms, lightning, and fire.

St. Bertulph the Abbot
Memorial: February 5

Born around 640, St. Bertulph converted to Christianity as a young man in Belgium. He migrated to Renty, France, where for many years he managed a farm for a wealthy landowner. He became a priest after making a pilgrimage to Rome, and subsequently founded a monastery, where he served as abbot until his death around 705. One day, while St. Bertulph was at prayer in the fields, a fierce thunderstorm swept in and overtook the land. An eagle miraculously appeared, spread his generous wings, and shielded the saint, who continued his prayers undisturbed.

St. Cataldus of Taranto
Memorial: May 10

While some accounts say that St. Cataldus was shipwrecked in Taranto in southern Italy on his way to Jerusalem, other accounts state that following his pilgrimage to Jerusalem, he was inspired to reinvigorate the faith of wayward Christians in Taranto. This account has him boarding a ship on a fair day that quickly turned deadly when a violent storm struck. St. Cataldus lifted his eyes to heaven, prayed, and made the sign of the cross over the billowing waves. At once the seas grew calm. Having witnessed the miraculous power of his faith, many of his shipmates were converted. They landed safely not far from their intended port, and St. Cataldus eventually reached Taranto on foot, evangelizing along the way. The people of Taranto chose this humble, holy man to be their bishop.

See also page 162.

St. Donatus of Münstereifel
Memorial: June 30

Having received a Christian upbringing in Rome in the second century, St. Donatus had a successful career as a soldier in the Roman legion, rising to the rank of captain. In the year 166, while fighting along the banks of the Danube River, his unit was cut off from critical supplies by the enemy. While his Roman brothers-in-arms pleaded to their pagan gods, St. Donatus, whose devotion to Christ was kept secret lest he be executed for his faith, rallied all the other clandestine Christians in his unit to pray for help and for victory against the enemy. Their prayers were answered by a blinding rain and lightning storm that drove back the enemy. The Romans were able to seize much needed food, water, and other provisions and emerged victorious. However, around the year 180, St. Donatus was exposed as a Christian when he refused to marry the emperor's pagan granddaughter.

St. Donatus was buried in the St. Agnes catacomb outside of Rome, where his relics were discovered in 1646. During their enshrinement in 1652 in Münstereifel, Germany, a driving rainstorm ended abruptly as the procession of the relics began. At the conclusion of the enshrinement Mass, lightning struck the church, felling candles and igniting the priest's vestments. The priest cried out to St. Donatus and the flames were immediately extinguished, leaving no trace of harm.

See also page 118.

St. Erasmus/Elmo
Memorial: June 2

Genteel by birth and disposition, St. Erasmus was born in the latter part of the third century. He served as the first bishop of Antioch, and became a holy and gifted missionary preacher in Campania, Italy, which was under the jurisdiction of the Roman emperor Diocletian. There, he shared the gospel and converted many pagans to the faith. The emperor, enraged by St. Erasmus's refusal to disavow his God, ordered him to suffer many bitter and violent torments that increased in cruelty each time the saint professed his faith. However, at every turn, angels would appear to free St. Erasmus from being tortured, spare him from harm, or make him whole, after which he would resume preaching throughout the land. During one torture, a great electrical storm arose as St. Erasmus praised God loudly even though his mouth was full of pitch and oil. The furnace he was sitting on—as well as his tormenters and hecklers—all burned away, but St. Erasmus emerged without injury. He continued to endure many more persecutions under the reign of the Roman emperor Maximin, driving the emperor near to insanity with his miraculous resilience. St. Erasmus continued to preach and perform miracles, converting thousands more. He was called home by God at the hour of God's choosing—not his tormenter's—and was accorded the crown of a martyr around 303. He is one of the Fourteen Holy Helpers, and the shining lights in the sky that accompanied his death are known, especially by sailors, as an electrostatic phenomenon called St. Elmo's Fire.

St. Gratus of Aosta
Memorial: September 7

According to legend, St. Gratus, a fifth-century Italian bishop who was known for his great charity to the poor as well as for working miracles, was born into a noble family, studied at Athens, and became a monk. He traveled to Rome, where he experienced a vision at the former Parthenon, which led him to evangelize at Aosta. While there, he converted thousands and became its bishop. He is said to have been directed by God to the Holy Land to recover the head of St. John the Baptist. He encountered a violent storm during that journey. However, at the sound of his prayers, offered as he raised his arms to the sky, the storm miraculously subsided. He succeeded in finding the head of St. John the Baptist at the bottom of a deep well in Herod's palace. He smuggled the relic back to Aosta, where church bells are said to have rung by themselves, and two children were raised from the dead upon his entry. St. Gratus died of natural causes around 470 in Aosta.

See also pages 12 and 151.

St. Magnus of Füssen
Memorial: September 6

The wooden crosier of St. Magnus was said to be made of wood from the hazel tree. According to German lore, it was common practice for farmers to cut a twig of hazel and, during the first thunderstorm, fashion a wooden cross from the twig and place it as protection over the fields of grain. It may be that St. Magnus's powerful hazelnut staff provided the same kind of protection in warding off lightning strikes.

See also pages 10–11.

St. Scholastica
Memorial: February 10

Born in 480 in Italy, St. Scholastica was the twin sister of St. Benedict of Nursia (the Father of Western Monasticism). She is one of the most well known saints invoked for safety against storms and lightning. She became a nun at a convent in Subiaco, near her beloved brother's monastery. When St. Benedict founded a monastery in Monte Cassino, near Naples, she followed his example and moved her monastery about five miles away.

Even though the siblings were very close and felt great affection for one another, St. Benedict enforced strict visitation rules that limited their reunions to one each year at a farmhouse halfway between their monasteries. At their annual meeting in 543, following a day of delightful conversation and a delicious dinner, St. Scholastica got tears in her eyes as her brother and his traveling companions prepared to depart. She begged him to stay a while longer and continue the lively discourse on spiritual matters, which she so enjoyed. Her brother refused, citing the resoluteness of the Rule he had established and would not violate. She hung her head and prayed. To the astonishment of all, a terrific thunderstorm broke out that prevented anyone from leaving. When her brother reproached her, she replied, "I asked a favor of you, and you refused it. I asked it of Almighty God, and he has granted it me." At daybreak, the storm subsided, and the siblings parted. Three days later, as St. Benedict was praying in his cell, he had a vision of a white dove ascending into heaven, and knew it was the soul of his sister, who had just died. She was buried in a tomb he had prepared for himself; upon his death, he was buried beside her.

St. Thomas Aquinas
Memorial: January 28

Born into a large, noble family in 1225 in Aquino, Italy, St. Thomas Aquinas was left with a deeply ingrained fear of thunderstorms after the youngest of his sisters was struck and killed by lightning as they lay sleeping in the same room. He was educated at the Benedictine Monte Cassino Abbey and, at the age of nineteen, joined the Order of Preachers, founded by St. Dominic. His family, while not opposed to a religious vocation for their son, disapproved of his joining an order deeply committed to a life of poverty, and so they kidnapped him. They kept him confined to their home for two years, after which time they relented and permitted him to rejoin the order. He was ordained a priest at the University of Cologne.

St. Thomas's natural humility and quiet reserve gave him the nickname "the dumb ox," but his professor rightly predicted that he would one day "make his lowing heard to the ends of the earth." Indeed, the saint's prolific contribution of theological commentaries, arguments, and teachings, as well as his profound personal holiness, led to him being proclaimed a doctor of the church in 1567. Shortly before his death at the age of fifty, it was observed that the Lord spoke to him from a crucifix, saying, "Thomas, you have written well of me. What reward can I give you for all your labors?" The humble saint replied, "Nothing, Lord. Nothing but You."

St. Tibertius of Rome
Memorial: April 14

A third century convert to Christianity and the brother of St. Valerian, this Roman noble was brought to the faith by St. Cecilia, the wife of St. Valerian, and was baptized by Pope St. Urban I. He and his brother were imprisoned for their faith during the reign of the Roman emperor Severus in 229, and, along with their jailer, Maximus, who declared himself a Christian because of their courageous example, were put to death. A powerful storm broke out at the moment of their executions, leading to their association as protectors against stormy weather.

St. Victor of Marseilles
Memorial: July 21

A third-century Christian officer in the Roman army in Marseilles, France, St. Victor was vocal both in denouncing idol worship and encouraging fellow Christians. When word of his allegiance to Christ reached the ears of Roman authorities, he was taken prisoner and tortured multiple times. Around 290, he was put to death. Three Roman soldiers who were assigned to guard him and who were inspired to convert during St. Victor's imprisonment were also put to death. His body was buried in a cave, and an abbey was erected over his crypt.

An ancient statue of the Blessed Mother known as Our Lady the Green One (referring to the color of the mantle Our Lady wore) is venerated at the Abbey of St. Victor in Marseilles. During Candlemas Day on February 2, pilgrims process to the statue carrying blessed, lit, green-wax candles. The pilgrims use these same candles as protection of their homes and stables against lightning throughout the following year. This procession is duplicated using white candles on the Feast of the Assumption, which occurs at a time of year when sultry summer days can give rise to dangerous thunderstorms. Given that these processions take place at the Abbey of St. Victor, St. Victor is said to share in Our Lady's protection of the faithful.

St. Walburga
Memorial: February 25

Born in the eighth century, St. Walburga studied at a monastery in Dorset, England, where she later became a nun renowned for learning and holiness. In the mid-700s, she undertook a mission to evangelize and heal pagans in what is now Germany. Along the journey, the ship upon which she was sailing was overtaken by a terrible storm. St. Walburga knelt on the deck and prayed to God to deliver everyone from harm. The sea calmed immediately.

See also pages 82–83.

For Protection against Fire

St. Agatha of Sicily

Feast Day: February 5

A beautiful and pious young woman born to a noble family in Catania, Sicily, in the third century, St. Agatha was coveted as a bride by many. However, she rejected all her suitors for Christ. From the age of fifteen, she chose to wear the white robe and red veil *(flammeum)* of consecrated virgins. The Roman consul Quintianus became so enamored that he tried to blackmail her: if she would yield to him, he would make sure she was spared during the Roman emperor Decius's persecutions against Christians. She declined the offer. As punishment, he had her sent to a brothel, where she was able to resist being violated. Quintianus again confronted her, this time insisting that she make sacrifice to idols. When she refused, she was beaten, imprisoned, and racked. He then had her breasts cut off and threw her back into prison. Amid her terrible suffering, St. Peter is said to have appeared in her cell in a vision, and he restored her body to wholeness. The miracle did not dissuade the cruel Quintianus. She was brought before the tyrant, who ordered her body to be rolled over a bed of hot coals mixed with pot shards. As mockery, she was to be covered only by the red veil that signified her betrothal to Christ. As she was being tortured, a violent earthquake struck the city. The people of Catania, terrorized by the event, demanded that Quintianus stop tormenting the holy young woman. Fearing an uprising, Quintianus sent St. Agatha, now barely alive, back to prison where the Lord, hearing her prayers, received her soul on February 5, 251. The red veil in which she was wrapped miraculously suffered no harm, and was preserved by the faithful as a precious relic.

Precisely one year later, Mount Etna "erupted a great fire, and like a fiery river, so the fiery liquid, melting stones and earth, came to the city of Catania." The frightened citizens fled to St. Agatha's tomb to beg her intercession. They retrieved the holy veil and placed it in the path of the boiling lava, the flow of which was miraculously halted, thereby saving the city from destruction. Martyrdom on a bed of burning coals along with the fiery nature of lava has led the faithful to invoke St. Agatha for protection against the ravages of fire.

See also page 187.

St. Amabilis of Riom
Memorial: November 1

St. Amabilis was a third-century cantor in a church at Clermont, France, as well as a holy and humble parish priest in Riom, France. He was a miracle worker both in life and in death. Following his death in 475 of natural causes, his relics were carried every June 11 in procession throughout Riom, with miraculous cures occurring in their wake. Small ribbons rubbed against his bones by the townspeople were believed to help preserve homes from fire, thunder, and lightning.

A more recent report dating from 1889 states that a great fire raged through the city of Spokane, Washington, threatening to devour Our Lady of Lourdes Church, which sat in the center of the fire's thirty-two-block path. A nun rushed to fetch a relic of St. Amabilis of Riom, and gave it to a priest, who threw it into the fire. The church was miraculously saved from the conflagration but every brothel, house of gambling, and bar in the area was destroyed. The morning after the fire, the relic was found wholly intact. Images and medals of the saint always carry the inscription, "The devil fled, as well as the serpent and the fire."

St. Amabilis of Riom is also known as St. Amabilis of Auvergne, whose feast day is October 18.

St. Caesarius of Arles
Memorial: August 27

St. Caesarius at the age of eighteen was already a devout monk living in the fifth century in a monastery in Lérins, Gaul (modern France), where he was a caretaker of the wine cellar. For his virtue and prudence in managing and rationing the house wine, he was rewarded with the disapproval of his fellow monks.

When he took ill, he was transferred to Arles by his uncle, who served as the city's bishop. There, he became a priest, advanced in holiness, and in 503 became the bishop of Arles. For forty years he ruled over this see, becoming known as a great reformer, preacher, and teacher until a political misunderstanding with King Alaric II of the Visigoths resulted in punishment by exile to Bordeaux. A fire broke out one night during his exile, and the townspeople immediately came to him for intercession. St. Caesarius prostrated himself in prayer before the flames, and they were immediately extinguished. Soon after, he was recalled from exile to Arles, where he died in 543.

St. Catherine of Siena
Memorial: April 29

The twenty-third of twenty-five children born to Christian parents in 1347 in Siena, Italy, St. Catherine was among the most beautiful and most devout of her siblings. She practiced many mortifications, including a three-year period of extreme fasting and prayerful isolation, all while living at home. Her parents arranged many marriages for St. Catherine, but she rebuffed them all, wishing only to be espoused to Christ. After her father witnessed a white dove hovering over his daughter when she was at prayer, he finally relented and gave his blessing for her to enter religious life. At eighteen, she entered the Dominican Order as a tertiary. A bout of chicken pox scarred her face, for which she was glad, as her diminished beauty would presumably discourage would-be suitors.

She began to experience visions of heaven, purgatory, and hell, and received the gift of reading souls. She was eventually called out of seclusion by Christ to enter public ministry. She ministered to her large family, served the poor on the streets and in hospitals, counseled popes, and wrote hundreds of letters that detailed her visions and experiences of God. She was proclaimed a doctor of the church. She died at the age of thirty-three—the same age as our Lord—of a stroke, in 1380.

St. Catherine was fond of using the imagery of the divine fire, a symbol for the experience of union with God in contemplative prayer, and often referred to the image of burning coals, which enflame the soul with love of God. The saying *Be who God meant you to be and you will set the world on fire* is an adaptation of a line from one of her letters: "If you are what you ought to be, you will set fire to all Italy, and not only yonder."

St. Eustachius
Memorial: September 20

St. Eustachius, his wife, and two sons converted to Christianity after he heard the voice of Christ and saw a glowing cross during a hunting expedition. Prior to his conversion, St. Eustachius was an esteemed Roman general. When the Roman emperor Trajan learned of the conversion, St. Eustachius was stripped of wealth and position and was separated from his family. He suffered years of hardship working in obscurity as a field hand for his wages. At a time when barbarians were threatening to invade Rome, St. Eustachius was discovered working the fields by two Roman soldiers, who recognized him. He was known for being an excellent tactician, and he was needed then more than ever before, so Trajan recalled him to duty. Upon the saint's return to Rome, he was joyfully reunited with his wife and sons. Incredibly, after the barbarians were driven back, the Roman emperor Hadrian ordered Eustacius to make a sacrifice of thanksgiving to the Roman gods. When St. Eustachius refused, he and his family were thrown to lions, where they miraculously suffered no harm. In 188 they were then martyred by being roasted inside a bronze bull. Their bodies were recovered from the flames unscarred, giving rise to St. Eustachius's association as a protector against fire. He is one of the church's Fourteen Holy Helpers.

St. Florian of Lorch
Memorial: May 4

Among the miracles attributed to St. Florian is the extinguishing of a fire that threatened to burn an entire city to the ground using only a single bucket of water and a prayer.

See also pages 146 and 183.

St. Francis of Assisi
Memorial: October 4

Legend holds that in 1219, during the Fifth Crusade, St. Francis traveled to Egypt in the hopes of converting the sultan of Egypt. A four-week ceasefire enabled St. Francis to cross the Muslim lines of battle where, eager to prove the veracity of the gospel, he challenged Egypt's religious authorities to a "trial by fire." By some accounts, the challenge was accepted by the sultan, and St. Francis walked through a pit of fire unscathed.

See also pages 29 and 61.
See also pages 196-97 for St. Francis's "Canticle of the Sun".

St. Francis of Paola
Memorial: April 2

At the age of fifteen, St. Francis of Paola left his family in Calabria to live a life of severe abstinence and penance in a cave by the sea near Paola, Italy. Later, he was joined by other men who had also been called to religious life, and the order of the "Minims" (that is, the self-professed "least" of the monastic orders) was born around 1435.

The prayers of St. Francis worked miracles in healing the sick, averting the plague, performing exorcisms, and raising the dead. He also exercised a special pastoral care for the poor. Once, a famed preacher, at the prodding of a group of disgruntled monks, paid a visit to St. Francis for the purpose of gathering evidence to discredit him. Francis received him with humble hospitality, even as he listened to the preacher's charges of fraud against him. When the preacher finished speaking, St. Francis grabbed a handful of hot coals from the fire and said, "Come, warm yourself, for you are shivering for want of a little charity." When he opened his hand, there was no trace of any burns. The preacher immediately recognized his envy, repented, and became among St. Francis's greatest friends and supporters.

St. Francis became the comfort and counselor of French kings and high-office politicians, who conferred much favor and honor upon him. His fame as a holy man and miracle worker grew. Even so, he never lost touch with an authentic, profound humility. Though he never stopped longing to return to Italy, he spent the final twenty-five years of his life in France. He died on Good Friday in 1507 at the age of ninety-one.

St. Helen
Memorial: August 18

Best known as the mother of Constantine the Great, St. Helen was a third-century Christian convert who was cast off by her first husband, a co-regent of the Roman Empire who sought a more fortuitous political liaison with another woman. Upon her former husband's death in 308 and Constantine's ascension to the throne, she was welcomed back to the royal court by her son. She founded churches throughout the Roman Empire, and conducted an arduous search for the True Cross, which she discovered in Jerusalem in 326, when she was well into her eighties. She died in 330, and her remains reside in the Vatican Museum.

Her Christian faith, charity, and concern for the poor set a heroic example for her son, but his own conversion didn't take place until 312, when his empire was attacked by the powerful forces of the Roman emperor Maxentius. Faced with a crisis, Constantine knelt and prayed to his mother's Christian God for a sign of his presence and favor. A cross of fire, which was seen by his entire army, promptly appeared in the sky. Beneath the cross, written in Latin, were the words that meant, *Through this sign thou shalt conquer.* Constantine fashioned a cross in the likeness of the one in the sky, which his soldiers on the front line carried into battle. The victory was won. The cross of fire may explain the link between St. Helen and her protection against fire. But it was also her burning love of Christ that led her to discover the True Cross for the edification of the faithful, as perhaps it may have been her maternal prayers that sparked the cross of fire that saved the soul of her son.

St. Lawrence
Memorial: August 10

The manner of St. Lawrence's execution, which was to be grilled over gridirons, accounts for his assignment as a protector against fire. Tradition holds that the ashes of his body were scattered by the wind and appear around the world on his feast day.

See also pages 87–88 and 119–120.

St. Lucy of Syracuse
Memorial: December 13

When she was denounced as a Christian, St. Lucy, a late-first-century virgin martyr from Syracuse, Italy, was surrounded by a pile of kindling that was set ablaze. Miraculously, the flames did not harm her. After a series of torments that included the gouging of her eyes, she was martyred by the sword in 304.

See also page 80.

St. Marcellinus of Ancona
Memorial: January 9

A sixth-century bishop of Ancona, Italy, St. Marcellinus is said to have put out a blazing fire by waving his prayer book at the flames. Thereafter, people were cured of all kinds of maladies merely by holding his book while praying. Other accounts state that the bishop, who suffered from gout and was unable to walk, was carried on a stretcher to the scene of a raging fire that was threatening to destroy Ancona. As soon as the good bishop drew near, the flames subsided, and the city was spared. He died around 566 of natural causes.

St. Nicholas of Myra
Memorial: December 6

Legend holds that on the day of St. Nicholas's consecration as archbishop of Myra, a young mother was bathing her infant in a tub. The metal bathtub had been placed over a small fire to keep the bathwater warm, and when the church bells rang to announce the start of the ceremony, the young mother, in her elation, rushed to the cathedral to witness the great event. Upon returning home and being jarred to her senses at the sight of smoke throughout the house, she feared her baby had perished. Miraculously, the child was found unharmed, sitting in the tub as though nothing had happened. This was the first miracle attributed to St. Nicholas after he became a bishop. Many more followed and continued even after his death.

See also pages 80–81, 88–89, 110–11, 114, 121, 125, and 133–34.

For Protection against Flood

St. Christopher
Memorial: July 25

St. Christopher received instruction and baptism from a hermit. In imitation of the hermit, he sought to humbly serve the Lord. The hermit suggested, owing to his enormous size and great strength, that he carry wayfarers needing to cross the nearby high, swift-running river upon his broad shoulders. St. Christopher performed this task day and night. One day, he carried the Christ Child himself upon his shoulders. Inspired by this event, St. Christopher became a missionary preacher of the gospel and converted many thousands of people.

See also pages 104–05 and 132.

St. Columbanus
Memorial: November 23

Founder of the renowned abbey at Bobbio, Italy, in 614, St. Columbanus would never have become a monk if his Irish mother had her way. She blocked the door and forbade her handsome son to leave the house when he confessed his desire to renounce the world. Already well educated, he advanced in knowledge and wisdom as a monk. In 583, called to become a missionary, St. Columbanus sailed to Britain and then to France. He founded a monastery in France but was so deeply attached to the Irish traditions of monastic life that the rules of his new monastery met with opposition from the local bishops. He also alienated the French royal family over his moral stand on marriage, which the king had violated. The king had him exiled, whereupon St. Columbanus settled in northern Italy.

He was known for working miracles among the poor and sick as well as for his gift of prophecy. One of his better-known predictions states that there will occur an end-time flood in Ireland that will obliterate the land.

Modern scientists agree that Ireland would be catastrophically affected by a mega-tsunami generated by the collapse of the volcano *Cumbre Vieja* in the Canary Islands. This ominous prediction likely accounts for the saint's association with protection against floods.

St. Florian of Lorch
Memorial: May 4

St. Florian's martyrdom by drowning led to his adoption as a protector against drowning and other dangers from water, including flooding.

See also pages 146 and 179.

St. Gregory Thaumaturgus
Memorial: November 17

Born in the early third century in Asia Minor (modern Turkey), and christened "Theodore" by his wealthy, pagan parents, the man who would become St. Gregory received a superior education in law and rhetoric with the expectation that he would attend law school. However, that changed when Theodore met Origen, the head of a catechetical school in Egypt. Theodore and his brother both converted to Christianity, which is when Theodore changed his name to Gregory. He studied theology, was ordained, and became the bishop of Caesarea. He was known as a wonder worker, teacher, healer, and minister to the poor and sick, especially those stricken with the mid-third century plague. Among his many miracles was one of great significance involving the river Lycus, which frequently produced devastating floods that swept away people, cattle, houses, and crops. He planted his staff on the banks of the river and prayed that the river would not rise higher than the staff. As a sign his prayers had been heard, the staff rooted and was transformed into a magnificent tree, the boundary of which was never again breached by floodwaters. St. Gregory died around 270 of natural causes.

See also page 190.

St. Hermengild
Memorial: April 13

The son of an Arian king of the Visigoths, St. Hermengild married a Frankish Catholic princess in 576, received instruction in the faith, and converted to Christianity, which enraged his heretic father. After a failed military campaign against his father's Arian kingdom, St. Hermengild sought sanctuary in Cordova, Spain. Thereafter, he was enticed to a reconciliation between himself and his father, but it was all a ruse. St. Hermengild was stripped of his royal robes and position. In 584 he was banished to Valencia, where he was imprisoned in the Tower of Seville. It is said his father promised him forgiveness and release from prison if he would consent to accept Holy Communion from the hands of an Arian bishop. When St. Hermengild refused to do so, he was beheaded on Easter Day, 585. His relics remain in Seville, Spain, where massive city walls known as *murallas* dating from the twelfth century fortified Seville against enemy attacks and flooding from the river Guadalquivir. Throughout the centuries, the faithful have called upon St. Hermengild, the patron saint of Seville, for protection against floods, storms, and other natural disasters.

St. Margaret of Hungary
Memorial: January 18

The daughter of Hungarian royalty, St. Margaret was sent at the age of three to a Dominican convent in satisfaction of a promise made by her parents in exchange for the deliverance of Hungary from the invasion of the Mongols. By the age of ten she had been transferred to the Monastery of the Blessed Virgin near Budapest that had been founded by her parents. She spent the remainder of her life there, refusing the opportunity for a political marriage to the king of Bohemia.

She practiced severe self-mortifications and requested the most menial chores in the convent. Her austere lifestyle had such a destructive effect on her physical health, she died at the age of twenty-eight in 1270. Efforts to canonize her were swift since there were more than seventy-four miracles, including the raising of the dead, already attributed to her intercession. Among them is the story of a convent maid who, having fallen into a well, was saved from drowning by the prayers of St. Margaret. This likely contributed to her association against the dangers of water, including floods. Further, the convent built by her parents was situated on a small island in the middle of the Danube River. When rising water threatened to overtake the island, her prayers were said to have kept floodwaters at bay.

See also page 217 for a Blessing to Ward off Floods.

For Protection against Hailstorms

St. Barnabas the Apostle
Memorial: June 11

A first-century follower of Christ, St. Barnabas traditionally is said to be one of the seventy-two disciples commissioned by Jesus to preach the gospel. Born in Cyprus, he is mentioned repeatedly in the Acts of the Apostles, and was a frequent traveling companion of St. Paul. With St. Paul, he founded the church in Antioch. He was stoned to death in Cyprus in 61 by the Jews for his success in winning souls for Christ. Owing to the manner of his death by stoning, he is invoked for protection against hailstorms.

St. John the Apostle
Memorial: December 27
Legend states that when St. John denounced the idol worship of the pagan goddess Artemis, her followers intended to stone him to death. However, the stones miraculously boomeranged, striking his assailants instead. This incident led to St. John's association with protection against hailstorms.

See also pages 87, 119, and 147.

St. John the Baptist
Memorial: June 24
In the Como and Milan regions of Italy, an annual festival known as the *Sagra de San Giovanni* takes place on the weekend closest to St. John's feast day. The ancient festival commemorates that legendary day when residents implored St. John the Baptist for his help in warding off the devastating June hailstorms that threatened their harvest each year. They boarded their boats and made a solemn procession to the small church dedicated to the saint on the small island of Comacina, within Lake Como. There, they prayed for St. John's protection. The crops were never again damaged by hailstorms.

See also pages 56–57 and 85.

St. Paul the Apostle
Memorial: June 29
According to the Acts of the Apostles (14:19), Jews from Antioch and Iconium turned the crowds at Lystra against St. Paul and his teachings. He miraculously survived their stoning. As with St. Barnabas, this persecution led to his being invoked for protection against hailstorms and stones.

See also pages 17 and 100–01.

St. Romedio of Nonsburg

Memorial: January 15

Born into the family of the counts of Thaur (modern Austria), St. Romedio was taught to read as a young child by a clergyman who incorporated the Bible and the lives of the saints as teaching resources. The holy textbooks fostered a great devotion to Christ in the child, who would eventually dispense his inheritance to the local churches, convert his family castle into a monastery, and visit the tombs of the apostles. After he had accomplished all of this, he chose to live with two companions in a cave near Salzburg, where he gained a reputation as a kind and holy man whose prayers brought cures and helped the townspeople in their distress. He died in the mid-fifth century and was mourned by many devotees.

St. Romedio's relics are enshrined in both Austria and Italy, where towns-people hang his image on the exteriors of their homes as a means of protection. In South Tyrol, Italy, St. Romedio's intercession is sought for protection against violent hailstorms that devastate apple orchards and other fruit trees, and his prayers are a trusted line of defense.

For Protection against Earthquakes

St. Agatha of Sicily

Feast Day: February 5

Legend asserts that as St. Agatha lay near death on a bed of hot coals, a violent earthquake struck the area. Many buildings were destroyed, and two of the advisors of the Roman consul, Quintianus, who had ordered her to be tortured, were killed. The citizens interpreted the earthquake as a sign of God's wrath at the torturing, and so they rushed to Quintianus and demanded that it be ceased. This event led St. Agatha to be declared a patron saint against earthquakes.

See also pages 175–76.

St. Amatus of Nusco
Memorial: September 30

Born around 1003 in Nusco, Italy, St. Amatus was the son of wealthy parents who became a priest, then, in 1048, the first bishop of Nusco. As bishop, he restored decaying churches and helped build new churches. He also helped found religious houses, including the Benedictine monastery of Santa Maria in nearby Fondigliano, Italy. He died in 1093 of natural causes. Many miracles and healings have occurred at his tomb. His relics are enshrined at the Church of St. Stephen in Nusco, and he is the patron saint of his birthplace. As a native son, he is invoked against earthquakes, which are a recurring natural disaster in the Irpinia Mountains.

St. Castulus of Rome
Memorial: March 26

St. Castulus was a chamberlain (valet) of the Roman emperor Diocletian and the husband of St. Irene of Rome. He secretly sheltered Christians in his home, which was adjacent to the palace. He also organized religious services inside the palace, figuring that this was the least likely place that anyone would look for them. He was responsible for the conversion of many in Rome, bringing them to Pope St. Caius to be baptized. He was tortured—suspended by his thumbs no fewer than three times—and buried alive in a sand pit outside of Rome in 286. His relics were translated to a Benedictine monastery in Moosburg, Bavaria (Germany) in 1171. There, the Bavarian faithful appointed him their guardian against lightning strikes and the wildfires that resulted from them.

See also pages 53–54.

St. Emygdius
Memorial: August 5

A second-century barbarian who converted to Christianity, St. Emygdius of Trier, in Germany, evangelized throughout Germany and Rome, where he cured a paralytic and a blind man. His reputation for performing healing miracles grew to the point that the pagan Romans thought him to be the son of

Apollo—that is, until he destroyed pagan idols and altars at the Temple of Aesculapius. He was hastily appointed bishop by Pope Marcellinus and sent to Ascoli Piceno to evangelize the region. Along the way, he won many converts, including the daughter of a local Roman governor named Polymius. In retaliation, Polymius had him beheaded in 303. The relics of St. Emygdius were enshrined at a church in Ascoli Piceno.

In 1703, a powerful earthquake struck the area encompassing the city of Ascoli Piceno, but the city itself was left virtually intact. The townspeople attributed this remarkable outcome to the protection of St. Emygdius. From then on, he was appointed as their protector against earthquakes, a designation that spread throughout Italy and all the way to the earthquake-prone American cities of Los Angeles and San Francisco. His patronage spread to the Monterey Diocese in California following the great Fort Tejon quake in 1857. In 1863, his influence expanded to Los Angeles.

St. Francis Borgia
Memorial: October 10

Born in 1510, the son of a long line of illustrious Spanish nobles, St. Francis demonstrated great virtues from a young age. He was a devout Catholic when he married a fellow noble, Eleanor de Castro. He fathered eight children, and when his wife died in 1546, his long-held admiration for St. Ignatius of Loyola, founder of a new religious order, ordained his next profession. After making provisions for his family, he entered the Society of Jesus, studied for the priesthood, and was ordained. In 1554, St. Ignatius named him the commissary general of the Jesuits in Spain and Portugal, and in 1565, he was made the father-general of the entire Jesuit order. This Duke-turned-Jesuit built hospitals, established monasteries, aided the poor, and introduced a mandatory daily meditation hour to Jesuit spirituality. He died in 1571 of natural causes. Pope Benedict XIV proclaimed St. Francis a patron saint against earthquakes in 1756, after approximately fifty thousand people perished during an earthquake in Lisbon, Portugal.

St. Gregory Thaumaturgus
Memorial: November 17

St. Gregory's command over the natural landscape led to his association with protection against earthquakes and other natural calamities. Upon leaving his eremitical life to minister to the people of Neocaesarea, a church was hastily constructed, to which the people gladly contributed their money and labor. Though many such churches were destroyed under the Roman emperor Diocletian's persecutions, and subsequent earthquakes in the region demolished many of the surrounding buildings, not one stone of the little church was thrown to the ground. Legend states that when the church was being built, St. Gregory commanded a giant boulder that stood in the way of their work to yield its place, which it did. St. Gregory Thaumaturgus died around 270 of natural causes.

See also pages 183–84.

St. Ponziano of Spoleto
Memorial: January 19

A young man born to a noble family in Spoleto, Italy, around 156, St. Ponziano was denounced as a Christian and brought before the Roman authorities during the reign of the Roman emperor Marcus Aurelius. Though only eighteen, the brave Christian preferred to suffer martyrdom rather than renounce his faith. Before being beheaded, St. Ponziano predicted that "Spoleto will shake but will not collapse." When a series of catastrophic earthquakes struck on his feast day in 1703 and continued throughout Italy for three weeks, killing thousands, Spoleto was spared the worst of the damage and not a single soul perished.

———

Part V

Blessings and Prayers

For the Day

The Angelus

The Angelus prayer is thought to have its genesis in Italy as early as the eleventh century, arising from the Franciscan monastic custom of reciting three Hail Marys around the time of sunset (6:00 p.m.), after evening vespers. The morning (6:00 a.m.) and midday (12:00 p.m.) prayers were later introduced but were common-place throughout Europe by the first half of the fourteenth century. Sometime in the sixteenth century, three sentences ("versicles") were added to each of the daily recitations to form the Angelus prayer as it's known today. Morning, noon, and night, the bells of monasteries and churches would ring three times, calling the faithful to cease all activity to pray and contemplate the mystery of the Incarnation as announced to the Blessed Virgin Mary by the angel Gabriel. It is said that even the plough animals would stop in their tracks at the first stroke of the Angelus bell.

The ringing of the bell itself is distinct: three strokes, followed by a pause and a series of nine strokes. Fifteenth-century records indicate the bell ringer of old was directed to "toll the Ave-bell nine strokes at three times, keeping the space of one Pater and Ave between each of the three tollings."

In Catholic villages across Europe, farmworkers were among those who would pause from their labors as the Angelus bells rang to meditate on the life, death, and resurrection of Christ, as well as on their own salvation. This sacred pause is captured in the renowned painting by French artist Jean-Francois Millet titled The Angelus *(1857–1859). The artist himself grew up on a family farm in a tiny hamlet in northwest France, and though he later studied and refined his art in Paris for twelve years, he eventually returned to the countryside where his heart was most at peace, declaring, "A peasant I was born and a peasant I will die."*

The painting expresses the artist's vivid memories of his own parents halting their work in the fields at the sound of the evening Angelus bell—his pious father clutching his cap in his rough hands and his mother bowing her weary head in prayer. The faith, dignity, and humility of rural farmers everywhere are immortalized in an intimate scene that couples soft, fading light with the harsh realities and tools of a farmer's daily life: a pitchfork, a wheelbarrow, a half-full harvest basket, and a vast field of crops yet to be picked. In the distant background, a silhouette of the church steeple from which the bells toll pierces a dusky sky.

As the story goes, when Millet's agent saw the painting displayed on the easel for the first time, the artist turned to him and asked, "Well, what do you think of it?"

"It is the Angelus," the agent replied.

"Yes," Millet said and nodded pensively. "Can you hear the bells?"

The Angelus

> V: The Angel of the Lord declared unto Mary,
> R: And she conceived of the Holy Spirit.
> Hail Mary . . .
>
> V: Behold the handmaid of the Lord,
> R: Be it done unto me according to your Word.
> Hail Mary . . .
>
> V: And the Word was made flesh,
> R: And dwelt among us.
> Hail Mary . . .
>
> V: Pray for us, O holy Mother of God,
> R: That we may be made worthy of the promises of Christ.
> Let us pray.

Pour forth, we beseech you, O Lord, your grace into our hearts: that we, to whom the Incarnation of Christ your Son was made known by the message of an Angel, may by his Passion and Cross be brought to the glory of his Resurrection. Through the same Christ our Lord. Amen.

The Angelus Bell

FIRST CHILD MORNING
Hail, Mary! Now the sun is up
   All things around look glad and bright,
And heather-bell and butter-cup
   Shake off the dew-drops of the night.
The lambs are frisking in the fields,
   The lark is singing in the sky;
And man his waking tribute yields
   To thee and thy sweet Son on high.

SECOND CHILD NOON
Hail, Mary! midway in the sky
   The noontide sun its lustre sheds,
The field-flowers almost seem to die,
   So low they hang their drooping heads.
The lambs have sought the woodland shade.
   The lark has ceased her note of glee;
And pausing in the furrowed glade,
   The ploughman lifts his heart to thee.

THIRD CHILD EVENING
Hail, Mary! now the sun is far
   Adorn his western path of light,
The flowers, beneath the evening star,
   Drink up the dew-drops of the night.
The lambs are by their mothers laid,
   The lark is brooding o'er her nest,
And when the evening prayer is made,
   Then weary man shall sink to rest.

—The Metropolitan Second Reader, 1883

St. Francis's Canticle of the Sun

O most High, almighty, good Lord God,
        to you belong praise, glory, honor, and all blessing!

Praised be my Lord God with all creatures;
and especially our brother the sun,
which brings us the day, and the light;
fair is he, and shining with a very great splendor:
O Lord, he signifies you to us!

Praised be my Lord for our sister the moon,
and for the stars,
which God has set clear and lovely in heaven.

Praised be my Lord for our brother the wind,
and for air and cloud, calms and all weather,
by which you uphold in life all creatures.

Praised be my Lord for our sister water,
which is very serviceable to us,
and humble, and precious, and clean.

Praised be my Lord for brother fire,
through which you give us light in the darkness:
and he is bright, and pleasant, and very mighty,
and strong.

Praised be my Lord for our mother the Earth,
which sustains us and keeps us,
and yields diverse fruits,
and flowers of many colors, and grass.

Praised be my Lord for all those who pardon
one another for God's love's sake,
and who endure weakness and tribulation;
blessed are they who peaceably shall endure,
for you, O most High, shall give them a crown!

Praised be my Lord for our sister,
the death of the body,
from which no one escapes.

Woe to him who dies in mortal sin!
Blessed are they who are found walking
by your most holy will,
for the second death shall have no power
to do them harm.

Praise you, and bless you, my Lord,
and give thanks to God,
and serve God with great humility.

Prayer Invoking St. Isidore the Farmer

Lord God, to whom belongs all creation, and who call us to serve you by
caring for the gifts that surround us, inspire us by the example of Saint Isidore
to share our food with the hungry and to work for the salvation of all people.
Through our Lord Jesus Christ, your Son, who lives and reigns with you in
the unity of the Holy Spirit, one God for ever and ever.

—The Roman Missal of the Catholic Church,
From the Common of Holy Men and Women,
on the Feast Day of Saint Isidore.

Prayer to St. Joseph the Worker

O Glorious St. Joseph, model of all those who are devoted to labor, obtain for me the grace to work in a spirit of penance for the expiation of my many sins; to work conscientiously, putting the call of duty above my natural inclinations, to work with thankfulness and joy, in a spirit of penance for the remission of my sins, considering it an honor to employ and develop by means of labor the gifts received from God, to work with order, peace, moderation, and patience, never shrinking from weariness and trials, to work above all with purity of intention and detachment from self, keeping unceasingly before my eyes death and the account that I must give of time lost, of talents unused, good omitted, and vain complacency in success, so fatal to the work of God. All for Jesus, all through Mary, all after thine example, O Patriarch, St. Joseph. Such shall be my watchword in life and in death. Amen.

—Prayer of Pope Pius X

A Blessing of Anything

(Make the sign of the cross where the + sign appears.)

   P: Our help is in the name of the Lord.
   All: Who made heaven and earth.
   P: The Lord be with you.
   All: May He also be with you.

   Let us pray.

God, whose word suffices to make all things holy, pour out your blessing + on this object (these objects); and grant that anyone who uses it (them) with grateful heart and in keeping with your law and will, may receive from you, its (their) Maker, health in body and protection of soul by calling on your holy name; through Christ our Lord.
All: Amen.

It (they) is (are) sprinkled with holy water.

For the Animals

A Blessing of Animals

Blessed are you, Lord God, maker of all living creatures. You called forth fish in the sea, birds in the air, and animals on the land. You inspired Saint Francis to call them his brothers and sisters. We ask you to bless this pet, this animal. By the power of your love, enable it to live according to your plan. Blessed are you, Lord our God, in all your creatures! Amen.

(The animal is gently sprinkled with holy water.)

A Blessing of Sick Animals

The priest, vested in surplice and purple stole, says:

P: Our help is in the name of the Lord.
All: Who made heaven and earth.
P: Deal not with us, Lord, as our sins deserve.
All: Nor take vengeance on us for our transgressions.
P: You, O Lord, will save both men and beasts.
All: Just as you, O God, show mercy again and again.
P: You open your hand.
All: And fill every living creature with your blessing.
P: Lord, heed my prayer.
All: And let my cry be heard by you.
P: The Lord be with you.
All: May He also be with you.

Let us pray.

God, who supplied animals to lighten man's toil, we humbly entreat you to preserve these creatures, since without them we cannot subsist; through Christ our Lord.
All: Amen.

Let us pray.

We humbly entreat your mercy, O Lord, praying that in your name and by the power of your blessing + these animals may be cured of the dire sickness that afflicts them. Let the devil's power over them be utterly abolished, and do you, Lord, protect their life and health against recurrent sickness; through Christ our Lord.
All: Amen.

Let us pray.

Have pity on us, Lord, we beg you, and turn away every scourge from your faithful. Rid our beasts of the dread sickness that is destroying them, so that we who are justly punished when we go astray may feel your gracious mercy when we repent; through Christ our Lord.
All: Amen.

(The sick animals are sprinkled with holy water.)
—Traditional Franciscan Prayer

A Blessing of Horses and Other Animals

P: Our help is in the name of the Lord.
All: Who made heaven and earth.
P: The Lord be with you.
All: May He also be with you.

Let us pray.

God, our refuge and our strength and source of all goodness, heed the holy prayers of your Church, and grant that we fully obtain whatever we ask for in faith; through Christ our Lord.
All: Amen.

Let us pray.

Almighty everlasting God, who helped the illustrious St. Anthony the Abbot to emerge unscathed from the many temptations that beset him in this world; help also your servants to grow in virtue by his noble example, and to be delivered from the ever-present dangers of this life by his merits and intercession; through Christ our Lord.
All: Amen.

Let us pray.

Lord, let these animals have your blessing + to the benefit of their being, and by the intercession of St. Anthony the Abbot deliver them from all evil; through Christ our Lord.
All: Amen.

(The horses or animals are sprinkled with holy water.)

An Equestrian's Prayer to St. Anne

Good St. Anne, mother of the Blessed Virgin Mary and patroness of horseback riders, by your maternal prayers and merits before God, may we who love and ride horses be ever safe, ever wise, ever calm, ever gentle, and ever joyful in our equestrian pursuits and in caring for our equine friends. By your loving intercession, may our horses enjoy all the benefits of your prayers and protection. Dear St. Anne, obtain for us these favors and all the spiritual blessings we seek through Jesus Christ, our Lord. Amen.

—Andie Andrews Eisenberg

A Blessing of Cattle, Herds, and Flocks

P: Our help is in the name of the Lord.
All: Who made heaven and earth.
P: The Lord be with you.
All: May He also be with you.

Let us pray.

Lord God, King of heaven and earth, Word of the Father by whom were made all creatures destined for our sustenance; we beg you to look with favor on our lowly condition; and as you have given us assistance in our work and in our needs, so may you bless, + shield, and watch over these animals (this animal) with your mercy and heavenly care. And to us, your servants, be pleased to give everlasting grace together with creature needs, thus enabling us to praise and glorify and offer thanks to your holy name; through Christ our Lord. All: Amen.

(The animals are sprinkled with holy water.)

A Blessing of Fowl or Any Kind of Bird

P: Our help is in the name of the Lord.
All: Who made heaven and earth.
P: The Lord be with you.
All: May He also be with you.

Let us pray.

God, author of all nature, who, among the many created species, also brought forth winged creatures from the primeval waters for the use of mankind; from which Noah, on coming out of the Ark, offered you a pleasing holocaust; who commanded your people, delivered from Egypt through Moses, your servant, to eat these winged creatures, separating the clean from the unclean; we humbly entreat you to bless + and to sanctify this flesh of clean birds, so that all who eat thereof may be filled with your bounteous blessing, and may deserve to come to the feast of everlasting life; through Christ our Lord. All: Amen.

(The birds are sprinkled with holy water.)

A Blessing of Bees and Their Hive

P: Our help is in the name of the Lord.
All: Who made heaven and earth.
P: The Lord be with you.
All: May He also be with you.

Let us pray.

Lord God almighty, who made the heavens and the earth, and all living things in the air and on land for the use of mankind; who ordered, through the ministers of holy Church, that candles made from the industry of bees should be lighted during the solemn mystery in which the most sacred body and blood of Jesus Christ, your Son, is confected and consumed; send your holy blessing + upon these bees and these beehives, causing them to multiply and to produce and to be kept from harm, so that their yield of wax can be turned to your honor, to that of the Son and Holy Spirit, and to the veneration of the blessed Virgin Mary; through Christ our Lord.
All: Amen.

(The bees and hives are sprinkled with holy water.)

Prayer to St. Anthony for Lost Animals

Dear St. Anthony, please come around,
[insert animal's name]
is lost and cannot be found!
—Traditional Catholic Prayer

Deprecatory Blessing against Pests

The priest, vested in surplice and a purple stole, comes to the field or place of infestation and says:

O God, our ears have heard, our fathers have declared to us.

—Psalm 43:1

All: Glory be to the Father.
P: As it was in the beginning.
All: Arise, Lord, help us; and deliver us for your kindness' sake.
P: Our help is in the name of the Lord.
All: Who made heaven and earth.
P: Lord, heed my prayer.
All: And let my cry be heard by you.
P: The Lord be with you.
All: May He also be with you.

Let us pray.

We entreat you, Lord, be pleased to hear our prayers; and even though we rightly deserve, on account of our sins, this plague of mice (or locusts, worms, etc.), yet mercifully deliver us for your kindness' sake. Let this plague be expelled by your power, and our land and fields be left fertile, so that all it produces redound to your glory and serve our necessities; through Christ our Lord.
All: Amen.

Let us pray.

Almighty everlasting God, the donor of all good things, and the most merciful pardoner of our sins; before whom all creatures bow down in adoration, those in heaven, on earth, and below the earth; preserve us sinners by your might, that whatever we undertake with trust in your protection may meet with success by your grace. And now as we utter a curse on these noxious pests, may they be cursed by you; as we seek to destroy them, may they be destroyed by you; as we seek to exterminate them, may they be exterminated by you; so that delivered from this plague by your goodness, we may freely offer thanks to your majesty; through Christ our Lord.
All: Amen.

For the Land

Prayer for the Renewal of the Earth

Bless the Lord, my soul!
  Lord, my God, you are great indeed!
You are clothed with majesty and splendor,
  robed in light as with a cloak.
You spread out the heavens like a tent;
  setting the beams of your chambers upon the waters.
You make the clouds your chariot;
  traveling on the wings of the wind.
You make the winds your messengers;
  flaming fire, your ministers.
You fixed the earth on its foundation,
  so it can never be shaken.
The deeps covered it like a garment;
  above the mountains stood the waters.
At your rebuke they took flight;
  at the sound of your thunder they fled.
They rushed up the mountains, down the valleys
  to the place you had fixed for them.
You set a limit they cannot pass;
  never again will they cover the earth.
You made springs flow in wadies
  that wind among the mountains.
They give drink to every beast of the field;
  here wild asses quench their thirst.
Beside them the birds of heaven nest;
  among the branches they sing.
You water the mountains from your chambers;
  from the fruit of your labor the earth abounds.
You make the grass grow for the cattle
  and plants for people's work
  to bring forth food from the earth,

wine to gladden their hearts,
   oil to make their faces shine,
   and bread to sustain the human heart.
The trees of the Lord drink their fill,
   the cedars of Lebanon, which you planted.
There the birds build their nests;
   the stork in the junipers, its home.
The high mountains are for wild goats;
   the rocky cliffs, a refuge for badgers.
You made the moon to mark the seasons,
   the sun that knows the hour of its setting.
You bring darkness and night falls,
   then all the animals of the forest wander about.
Young lions roar for prey;
   they seek their food from God.
When the sun rises, they steal away
   and settle down in their dens.
People go out to their work,
   to their labor till evening falls.
How varied are your works, Lord!
   In wisdom you have made them all;
   the earth is full of your creatures.
There is the sea, great and wide!
   It teems with countless beings,
   living things both large and small.
There ships ply their course
   and Leviathan, whom you formed to play with.
All of these look to you
   to give them food in due time.
When you give it to them, they gather;
   when you open your hand, they are well filled.
When you hide your face, they panic.
   Take away their breath, they perish
   and return to the dust.
Send forth your spirit, they are created
   and you renew the face of the earth.

—Psalm 104:1–30

A Blessing of Orchards and Vineyards

P: Our help is in the name of the Lord.
All: Who made heaven and earth.
P: The Lord be with you.
All: May He also be with you.

Let us pray.

Almighty God, we appeal to your kindness, asking that you pour out the dew of your blessing + on these budding creatures of yours, which it has pleased you to nurture with rain and mild breezes, and that you bring the fruits of your earth to a ripe harvest. Grant to your people a spirit of constant gratitude for your gifts. And from a fertile earth all the hungry with an abundance of good things, so that the poor and needy may praise your wondrous name forever and ever.
All: Amen.

(The orchards or vineyards are sprinkled with holy water.)

A Blessing of Fields, Mountain-Meadows, and Pastures

P: Our help is in the name of the Lord.
All: Who made heaven and earth.
P: The Lord be with you.
All: May He also be with you.

Let us pray.

God, from whom every good has its beginning and from whom it receives its increase, we beg you to hear our prayers, so that what we begin for your honor and glory may be brought to a happy ending by the gift of your eternal wisdom; through Christ our Lord.
All: Amen.

Let us pray.

Almighty everlasting God, who conferred on your priests above all others so great a grace, that whatever they do worthily and exactly in your name, is regarded as being done by you; we pray that in your kindness you may be present wherever we are present and may bless + whatever we bless. And at our lowly coming, through the merits and prayers of your saints, may demons flee and the angel of peace be at hand; through Christ our Lord.

All: Amen.

Now the Litany of the Saints is said; all kneel. After the following invocation: (That you deliver our souls and the souls of our brethren, relatives, and benefactors from everlasting damnation, and so on), the priest rises and says:

P: That you bless + these fields (or acres, or mountain-meadows, or pastures, or meadows).

All: We beg you to hear us.

P: That you bless + and consecrate + these fields (or acres, or mountain-meadows, or pastures, or meadows).

All: We beg you to hear us.

P: That you bless + and consecrate + and protect from diabolical destruction these fields (or acres, or mountain-meadows, or pastures, or meadows).

All: We beg you to hear us.

P: That you mercifully ward off and dispel from this place all lightning, hail-storm, destructive tempests, and harmful floods.

All: We beg you to hear us.

Then the litany is resumed to the end, after which the priest says the Our Father.

P: And lead us not into temptation.

All: But deliver us from evil.

P: Send forth your Spirit and all things shall be recreated.

All: And you shall renew the face of the earth.

P: The Lord shall manifest His goodness.

All: And the earth shall yield her fruit.

P: Lord, heed my prayer.

All: And let my cry be heard by you.

P: The Lord be with you.

All: May He also be with you.

Let us pray.

Almighty God, we humbly appeal to your kindness, asking that you pour out the dew of your blessing + on these fields (or acres, or mountain-meadows, or pastures, or meadows), which it has pleased you to nurture with favorable weather. Grant to your people a spirit of constant gratitude for your gifts. Wipe out any infertility from this land, thus filling the hungry with an abundance of good things, so that the poor and the needy may praise your wondrous name forever and ever.
All: Amen.

(The fields are sprinkled with holy water.)

A Blessing of Seed and Seedlings

(on the Birthday of the Blessed Virgin Mary – September 8)

P: Our help is in the name of the Lord.
All: Who made heaven and earth.
P: The Lord be with you.
All: May He also be with you.

Let us pray.

Holy Lord and Father, almighty everlasting God, we ask and beseech you to look with merry countenance and fair eyes on these seeds and seedlings. And as you proclaimed to Moses, your servant, in the land of Egypt, saying: "Tell the children of Israel that when they enter the land of promise which I shall give them, they are to offer the first-fruits to the priests, and they shall be blessed"; so too at our request, O Lord, be merciful and pour out the blessing + of your right hand upon these seeds, which you in your benevolence bring forth to sustain life. Let neither drought nor flood destroy them, but keep them unharmed until they reach their full growth and produce an abundant harvest for the service of body and soul. We ask this of you who live and reign in perfect Trinity forever and ever.
All: Amen.

Let us pray.

Almighty everlasting God, sower and tiller of the heavenly word, who cultivate the field of our hearts with heavenly tools, hear our prayers and pour out abundant blessings upon the fields in which these seeds are to be sown. By your protecting hand turn away the fury of the elements, so that this entire fruit may be filled with your blessing, + and may be gathered unharmed and stored up in the granary; through Christ our Lord.
All: Amen.

(The seeds or seedlings are sprinkled with holy water and may also be incensed.)

A Blessing for Roses

O God, Creator and Preserver of the human race, who grant us the Holy Spirit with His seven-fold gifts, and who generously bestow eternal salvation: Sanctify, we pray, and bless these roses. We present them before You today, and seek Your blessing upon them, to express our thanks to You, and our devotion towards the blessed Ever-Virgin Mary and her Rosary. You created these roses as a source of pleasant fragrance and gave them to us to lift our spirits. Then through the power of the holy Cross pour out upon them Your heavenly + blessing. Signed by the holy + Cross may they receive so powerful a blessing that in the houses and hospitals where they are taken, the sick may be healed. From the places where they are kept, may the powers of evil flee in fear and terror, nor may they presume again to disturb Your servants. We ask this through Christ our Lord. Amen.

—Dominican Rite for the Blessing of Roses
From the Dominican Breviary, 1967

For the Farm

Blessing of a Home or Farmhouse

P: Our help is in the name of the Lord.
All: Who made heaven and earth.
P: The Lord be with you.
All: May He also be with you.

Let us pray.

Lord God almighty, bless + this home or farmhouse, that it be the shelter of health, purity, and self-control; that there prevail here a spirit of humility, goodness, mildness, obedience, and gratitude to God the Father, Son, and Holy Spirit. May this blessing remain on this place and on those who live here.
All: Amen.

(The home or farmhouse is sprinkled with holy water.)

Another Blessing of a Home or Farmhouse

P: Our help is in the name of the Lord.
All: Who made heaven and earth.
P: The Lord be with you.
All: May He also be with you.

Let us pray.

God the Father almighty, we fervently implore you for the sake of this home and its occupants and possessions, that you may bless + and sanctify + them, enriching them by your kindness in every way. Pour out on them heavenly dew, as well as an abundance of earthly needs. Mercifully listen to their prayers and be pleased to bless + and sanctify + this home. Within these walls let your angels of light preside and stand watch over those who live here; through Christ our Lord.
All: Amen.

(The home or farmhouse is sprinkled with holy water.)

The Blessing of a Stable for Horses, Cattle, and Other Animals

P: Our help is in the name of the Lord.
All: Who made heaven and earth.
P: The Lord be with you.
All: May He also be with you.

Let us pray.

Lord God almighty, who willed that your only-begotten Son, our Redeemer, be born in a stable, and lie in a manger between two beasts of burden; we beg you to bless + this stable and to defend it from all spite and wickedness of the devil. Let it be a healthful shelter for horses, cattle, and other animals, safe from every kind of assault. And as the ox knows his master and the ass the manger of his lord, so grant that your servants, made in your image and only a little lower than the angels, to whom you have subjected all sheep and oxen and cattle of the fields, may not be like senseless beasts, like the horse or the mule who are without understanding. But let them acknowledge you alone as God and the source of all good. Let them faithfully persevere in your service, show you gratitude for favors received, and thus merit greater benefits in the future; through Christ our Lord.
All: Amen.

(The stable and the animals therein are sprinkled with holy water.)

The Blessing of Crosses to Be Set in Fields and Vineyards

(Performed on the Feast of the Finding of the Holy Cross, September 14, or on the next Sunday.)

P: Our help is in the name of the Lord.
All: Who has made heaven and earth.
P: The Lord be with you.
All: And with your spirit.

Let us pray.

Almighty, everlasting God, Father of all consolation and kindness, through the merits of the bitter passion of your only Son, our Lord Jesus Christ, which he was so kind as to undergo for us sinners on the wood of the cross, bless these crosses, which your people will take from here to set in gardens, vineyards, fields, or other places, so that the farms on which they are set up may be free from the crushing of hail, the violence of tornadoes, the power of storms, and from every disturbance of the enemy. May then their produce be brought to full ripeness, and gathered in honor of your name by those who trust in the power of the holy cross of the same Jesus Christ, your Son, our Lord, who lives and is King with you for ever and ever.
All: Amen.

(The crosses are sprinkled with holy water.)

The Blessing of an Automobile, Wagon, or Tractor

P: Our help is in the name of the Lord.
All: Who has made heaven and earth.
P: The Lord be with you.
All: And with your spirit.

Let us pray.

Lend a willing ear, Lord God, to our prayers, and bless this vehicle with your holy right hand. Direct your holy angels to accompany it, that they may free those who ride in it from all dangers, and always guard them. And just as by your deacon Philip you gave faith and grace to the man of Ethiopia as he sat in his chariot reading the Sacred Word, so, point out to your servants the way of salvation. Grant that, aided by your grace, and with their hearts set on good works, they may, after all the joys and sorrows of this journey through life, merit to receive eternal joys, through Christ our Lord.
All: Amen.

(The automobile, wagon, or tractor is sprinkled with holy water.)

For Weather and Other Difficulties

A Prayer for Good Weather

Almighty ever-living God, who heals us through correction and saves us by your forgiveness, grant to those who seek your favor that we may rejoice at the good weather for which we hope, and always use what in your goodness you bestow for the glory of your name and for our well-being. Through our Lord Jesus Christ, your Son, who lives and reigns with you in the unity of the Holy Spirit, one God, for ever and ever. Amen.

—The Roman Missal of the Catholic Church, #36

A Prayer for Rain

O God, in whom we live and move and have our being, grant us sufficient rain, so that, being supplied with what sustains us in this present life, we may seek more confidently what sustains us for eternity. Through our Lord Jesus Christ, your Son, who lives and reigns with you in the unity of the Holy Spirit, one God, for ever and ever. Amen.

—The Roman Missal of the Catholic Church, #35

A Prayer for an End to Storms

O God, to whose commands all the elements give obedience, we humbly entreat you, that the stilling of fearsome storms may turn a powerful menace into an occasion for us to praise you. Through our Lord, Jesus Christ, your Son, who lives and reigns with you in the unity of the Holy Spirit, one God, for ever and ever. Amen.

—The Roman Missal of the Catholic Church, #37

A Prayer for Protection against Storms

Jesus Christ, a King of Glory, has come in Peace. + God became man, + and the Word was made flesh. + Christ was born of a virgin. + Christ suffered. + Christ was crucified. + Christ died. + Christ rose from the dead. + Christ ascended into Heaven. + Christ conquers. + Christ reigns. + Christ orders. + May Christ protect us from all storms and lightning. + Christ went through their midst in Peace, + and the Word was made Flesh. + Christ is with us with Mary. + Flee you enemy spirits because the Lion of the Generation of Juda, the Root David, has won. + Holy God! + Holy Powerful God! + Holy Immortal God! + Have mercy on us. Amen.

—This prayer originated in a convent and church in Lisbon, Portugal. It was ordered to be published by Pope Innocent, III, 1198-1216.

At a Time of Earthquake

O God, who set the earth on its firm foundation, spare those who are fearful and show favor to those who implore you, so that, with all dangers of earthquake entirely gone, we may continue to experience your mercy and serve you in thankfulness, safe under your protection. Through our Lord Jesus Christ, your Son, who lives and reigns with you in the unity of the Holy Spirit, one God, for ever and ever. Amen.

—The Roman Missal of the Catholic Church, #34

A Blessing to Ward off Floods

The priest, vested in surplice and stole, accompanied by the people, carries a relic of the True Cross to the river or stream, and there devoutly reads at each of four different spots one of the introductions to the four Gospels. After each Gospel he adds the following verses and prayers:

P: Help us, O God, our Savior.
All: And deliver us for your name's sake.
P: Save your servants.
All: Who trust in you, my God.
P: Deal not with us, Lord, as our sins deserve.
All: Nor take vengeance on us for our transgressions.
P: Lord, send us aid from your holy place.
All: And watch over us from Sion.
P: Lord, heed my prayer.
All: And let my cry be heard by you.
P: The Lord be with you.
All: May He also be with you.

Let us pray.

God, who gives saving grace even to the wicked land who do not will the death of the sinner, we humbly appeal to you in glory, asking that you protect with your heavenly aid your trusting servants from all perils of flood. Let them find in you a constant safeguard, so that they may always serve you and never be separated from you through any temptation; through Christ our Lord.
All: Amen.

And may the blessing of almighty God, Father, Son, + and Holy Spirit, come upon these waters and keep them always under control.
All: Amen.

The Blessing of a Well

P: Our help is in the name of the Lord.
All: Who made heaven and earth.
P: The Lord be with you.
All: May He also be with you.

Let us pray.

Lord God almighty, who so disposed matters that water comes forth from the depths of this well by means of its pipes, grant, we pray, that with your help and by this blessing + imparted through our ministry, all diabolical wiles and cunning may be dispelled, and the water of this well may always remain pure and wholesome; through Christ our Lord.
All: Amen.

(The well is sprinkled with holy water.)

For the Food

The Blessing of Eggs

P: Our help is in the name of the Lord.
All: Who made heaven and earth.
P: The Lord be with you.
All: May He also be with you.

Let us pray.

Lord, let the grace of your blessing + come upon these eggs, that they be healthful food for your faithful who eat them in thanksgiving for the resurrection of our Lord Jesus Christ, who lives and reigns with you for ever and ever.
All: Amen.

(The eggs are sprinkled with holy water.)

A Blessing of Cheese or Butter

P: Our help is in the name of the Lord.
All: Who made heaven and earth.
P: The Lord be with you.
All: May He also be with you.

Let us pray.

Lord God almighty, if it please you, bless + and sanctify + this cheese (or butter), which by your power has been made from the fat of animals. Grant that those of your faithful who eat it may be sated with a blessing from on high, with your grace and all good things; through Christ our Lord.
All: Amen.

(The cheese or butter is sprinkled with holy water.)

A Blessing of Salt or Oats for Animals

P: Our help is in the name of the Lord.
All: Who made heaven and earth.
P: The Lord be with you.
All: May He also be with you.

Let us pray.

Lord God, Creator and preserver of all things, in whose hand is the life and breath of every creature; we beg you to listen to the prayers of your faithful, and to pour out on this salt (or oats), your blessing + and the unseen working of your might. May the animals, which you have kindly given for the service of man, be spared every type of sickness when they eat this salt (or oats), and under your protection escape every affliction of hateful evil spirits; through Christ our Lord.
All: Amen.

(The salt or oats are sprinkled with holy water.)

A Blessing of Lard

(This blessing by modern association extends to bacon and other pork-fat products.)

P: Our help is in the name of the Lord.
All: Who made heaven and earth.
P: The Lord be with you.
All: May He also be with you.

Let us pray.

Lord, bless + this lard, and let it be a healthful food for mankind. Grant that everyone who eats it with thanksgiving to your holy name may find it a help in body and in soul; through Christ our Lord.
All: Amen.

(The lard is sprinkled with holy water.)

A Blessing of a Granary or the Harvest

P: Our help is in the name of the Lord.
All: Who made heaven and earth.
P: The Lord be with you.
All: May He also be with you.

Let us pray.

Lord God almighty, who never fails to bestow on men an abundance of heavenly gifts, as well as the rich fruits of the earth; we give thanks to you in your glory for this harvest of grain, and beg you again to bless + the harvest which we have received from your bounty, to preserve it and to shield it from harm. Grant also that, having had our desire for earthly needs filled, we may bask under your protection, praise your kindness and mercy without ceasing, and make use of temporal goods in such a way as not to lose everlasting goods; through Christ our Lord.
All: Amen.

(The granary or harvest is sprinkled with holy water.)

The Blessing of Seed

P: Our help is in the name of the Lord.
All: Who made heaven and earth.
P: The Lord be with you.
All: May He also be with you.

Let us pray.

Lord, we earnestly beg you to bless + these seeds, to protect and preserve them with gentle breezes, to make them fertile with heavenly dew, and to bring them, in your benevolence, to the fullest harvest for our bodily and spiritual welfare; through Christ our Lord.
All: Amen.

(The seed is sprinkled with holy water.)

A Blessing of Herbs

(To be prayed on the Assumption of the Blessed Virgin Mary – August 15)

With those assembled in the church holding herbs and fruits in their hands, the priest begins:

P: Our help is in the name of the Lord.

All: Who made heaven and earth.

Psalm 64 is read.

P: To you we owe our hymn of praise, O God, in Sion; to you must vows be fulfilled, you who hear prayers.

All: To you all flesh must come because of wicked deeds.

P: We are overcome by our sins; it is you who pardon them.

All: Happy the man you choose, and bring to dwell in your courts.

P: May we be filled with the good things of your house, the holy things of your temple.

All: With awe-inspiring deeds of justice you answer us, O God our Savior,

P: The hope of all the ends of the earth and of the distant seas.

All: You set the mountains in place by your power, you who are girt with might;

P: You still the roaring of the seas, the roaring of their waves and the tumult of the peoples.

All: And the dwellers at the earth's ends are in fear at your marvels; the farthest east and west you make resound with joy.

P: You have visited the land and watered it; greatly have you enriched it.

All: God's watercourses are filled; you have prepared the grain. Thus have you prepared the land:

P: Drenching its furrows, breaking up its clods,

All: Softening it with showers, blessing its yield.

P: You have crowned the year with your bounty, and your paths overflow with a rich harvest;

All: The untilled meadows overflow with it, and rejoicing clothes the hills.

P: The fields are garmented with flocks and the valleys blanketed with grain. They shout and sing for joy.

All: Glory be to the Father.

P: As it was in the beginning.

P: The Lord will be gracious.
All: And our land will bring forth its fruit.
P: You water the mountains from the clouds.
All: The earth is replenished from your rains.
P: Giving grass for cattle.
All: And plants for the benefit of man.
P: You bring wheat from the earth.
All: And wine to cheer man's heart.
P: Oil to make his face lustrous.
All: And bread to strengthen his heart.
P: He utters a command and heals their suffering.
All: And snatches them from distressing want.
P: Lord, heed my prayer.
All: And let my cry be heard by you.
P: The Lord be with you.
All: May He also be with you.

Let us pray.

Almighty everlasting God, who by your word alone brought into being the heavens, earth, sea, things seen and things unseen, and garnished the earth with plants and trees for the use of man and beast; who appointed each species to bring forth fruit in its kind, not only for the food of adversity from men and beasts who use them in your name; through Christ our Lord.
All: Amen.

Let us pray.

God, who through Moses, your servant, directed the children of Israel to carry their sheaves of new grain to the priests for a blessing, to pluck the finest fruits of the orchard, and to make merry before you, the Lord their God; hear our supplications, and shower blessings + in abundance upon us and upon these bundles of new grain, new herbs, and this assortment of produce which we gratefully present to you on this festival, blessing + them in your name. Grant that men, cattle, flocks, and beasts of burden find in them a remedy against sickness, pestilence, sores, injuries, spells, and against the fangs of serpents or poisonous creatures. May these blessed objects be a protection against diabolical mockery, cunning, and deception wherever they are kept, carried, or otherwise used. Lastly, through the merits of the blessed Virgin Mary, whose Assumption we are celebrating, may we all, laden with the sheaves of good works, deserve to be taken up to heaven; through Christ our Lord.

All: Amen.

The Blessing of St. John's Wine

(To be prayed on the feast of St. John, Apostle and Evangelist – December 27)

P: Our help is in the name of the Lord.
All: Who made heaven and earth.
P: The Lord be with you.
All: May He also be with you.

Let us pray.

If it please you, Lord God, bless + and consecrate + this vessel of wine (or any other beverage) by the power of your right hand; and grant that, through the merits of St. John, apostle and evangelist, all your faithful who drink of it may find it a help and a protection. As the blessed John drank the poisoned potion without any ill effects, so may all who today drink the blessed wine in his honor be delivered from poisoning and similar harmful things. And as they offer themselves body and soul to you, may they obtain pardon of all their sins; through Christ our Lord.

All: Amen.

Lord, bless + this creature drink, so that it may be a health-giving medicine to all who use it; and grant by your grace that all who taste of it may enjoy bodily and spiritual health in calling on your holy name; through Christ our Lord.

All: Amen.

May the blessing of almighty God, Father, Son, + and Holy Spirit, come on this wine (or any other beverage) and remain always.

All: Amen.

(The wine is sprinkled with holy water.)

A Blessing of Beer

P: Our help is in the name of the Lord.
All: Who made heaven and earth.
P: The Lord be with you.
All: May He also be with you.

Let us pray.

Lord, bless + this beer, which by your kindness and power has been produced from kernels of grain, and let it be a healthful drink for mankind. Grant that whoever drinks it with thanksgiving to your holy name may find it a help in body and in soul; through Christ our Lord.
All: Amen.

(The beer is sprinkled with holy water.)

A Blessing of Grapes

P: Our help is in the name of the Lord.
All: Who made heaven and earth.
P: The Lord be with you.
All: May He also be with you.

Let us pray.

Lord, bless + this new fruit of the vineyard, which in your benevolence you have ripened by heavenly dew, an abundance of rainfall, gentle breezes, and fair weather; and have given us to use with gratitude in the name of our Lord Jesus Christ, who lives and reigns with you, in unity of the Holy Spirit, God, forever and ever.
All: Amen.

(The grapes are sprinkled with holy water.)

A Blessing after the Harvest

O Lord, good Father, who in your providence have entrusted the earth to the human race, grant, we pray, that with the fruits harvested from it we may be able to sustain life and, with your help, always use them to promote your praise and the well-being of all. Through our Lord Jesus Christ, your Son, who lives and reigns with you in the unity of the Holy Spirit, one God, forever and ever. Amen.

—The Roman Missal of the Catholic Church, #28

Sources

Adels, Jill Haak. *The Wisdom of the Saints*. "St. Anthony of Padua." New York: Oxford University Press, 1987.

Archdiocese of Baltimore. "Setting the World on Fire: Inspiring Quotes from St. Catherine of Siena." Letter T368.https://www.archbalt.org/ setting-the-world-on-fire-inspiring-quotes-from-st-catherine-of-siena/.

Archives of the Lisieux Carmel, Last Conversations (LC 9.6, LC 17.7) https://www.archives-carmel-lisieux.fr/english/carmel/index.php/last-year-of-therese/ last-year-of-therese-page-3. Alternately, quoted text can be found in the book *My Vocation Is Love, Therese of Lisieux*, by Jean Lafrance. Originally published as *Ma vocation c'est l'amour* by Mediaspaul, 8 rue Madame 75006, Paris, France. English translation by Anne Marie Brennan OCD. © 1990, 1994 St. Pauls, Homebush NSW 2140, Australia, pages 9–10.

Benedict XVI. *St. Odo's Life*. September 2, 2009. https://anastpaul.com/2019/11/18/ saint-of-the-day-18-november-saint-odo-of-cluny-c-880-942/.

Breviary According to the Rite of the Order of Preachers, 1967.

Ford, David Nash. "St. Swithun, Bishop of Winchester." http://earlybritishkingdoms.com/adversaries/bios/swithun.html.

LaFrance, Jean. *My Vocation Is Love: St. Therese's Way to Total Trust*. Translated by Anne Marie Brennan, O.C.D. Boston: Pauline Books and Media, 2012.

Member of the Order of the Holy Cross. *The Metropolitan Second Reader: With Comprehension Activities*. Montreal: James A. Sadlier Catholic Publisher, 1883, 1993. https://www.crusaders-for-christ.com/uploads/8/9/4/8/8948848/ metropolitan_second_reader_-_with_comprehension_activities.pdf.

New American Bible. rev. ed. Washington, D.C.: Confraternity of Christian Doctrine, 2010, 1991, 1986, 1970.

The Roman Missal © 2010, International Commission on English in the Liturgy Corporation.

Roten, Fr. Johann G., S.M. "The Angelus: An Artistic Rendering." All about Mary. https://udayton.edu/imri/mary/a/angelus-painting-by-millet.php.

Scudder, Vida Dutton, ed. and trans. "To Stefano Maconi." Letters T329, T368. *St. Catherine of Siena as Seen in Her Letters*. London, New York: J. M. Dent and E. P. Dutton, 1905. http://www.domcentral.org/trad/cathletters.htm#2StefanoMaconi.

Stokes, John S., Jr. "Blessing Mary Gardens: The Blessing of Mary Gardens as Holy Places." https://udayton.edu/marianlibrary/marysgardens/b/blessing-mary-gardens.php.

Thérèse of Lisieux. *Story of a Soul: The Autobiography of St. Thérèse of Lisieux*. Translated by John Clarke, O.C.D. 3rd ed. Washington, DC: ICS Publications, 1996.

Thurston, Herbert. "Angelus Bell." *Catholic Encyclopedia*. Vol. 1. New York: Robert Appleton Company, 1907. https://www.newadvent.org/cathen/01487a.htm.

Thurston, Herbert J., SJ, and Donald Attwater, eds. *Butler's Lives of the Saints*. Westminster, MD: Christian Classics, 1990.

United States Conference of Catholic Bishops. *Resources for Liturgy: On Caring for God's Creation*. Washington, DC: USCCB, 2015. https://www.usccb.org/issues-and-action/human-life-and-dignity/environment/upload/ecology-resource-liturgy.pdf.

University of Notre Dame. "St. Thomas Aquinas." http://faith.nd.edu/s/1210/faith/interior.aspx?cid=27402&crid=0&ecid=27402&gid=609&pgid=13038&sid=1210.

Velez, Fr. Juan. "Mary, Mystical Rose." https://www.cardinaljohnhenrynewman.com/mary-mystical-rose-cardinal-newman/.

Voragine, Jacobus de, comp. 1275. *The Golden Legend* (Aurea legenda). Vol. 7. Translated by William Caxton, 1483.

Weller, Philip T., S.T.D., trans. "The Blessings." *Rituale Romanum* (Roman Ritual). Vol. 3. Milwaukee, WI: The Bruce Publishing Company, 1946.

Saints and Their Patronages

St. Abdon and St. Sennen
For the Protection of Gardeners

St. Achahildis of Wendelstein
For the Protection of Geese

Adam the Patriarch
For the Protection of Gardeners

St. Adelard of Corbie
For the Protection of Gardeners

St. Adrian of Nicomedia
For the Protection of Butchers

St. Agatha of Sicily
For Protection against Fire
For Protection against Earthquakes

St. Agnes of Rome
For the Protection of Gardeners
For the Protection of the Harvest

St. Agricola of Avignon
For Rain and Protection against Drought

St. Agrippina of Rome
For Protection against Storms and Lightning

St. Ailbe of Emly
For Protection against Wolves

Bl. Albert of Bergamo
For the Protection of Laborers

St. Amabilis of Riom
For Protection against Fire

St. Amand of Maastricht
For the Protection of Vintners
For the Protection of Grocers and Farmstands

St. Amatus of Nusco
For Protection against Earthquakes

St. Ambrose of Milan
For the Protection of Geese
For the Protection of Bees
For the Protection of Beekeepers

St. Andrew the Apostle
For the Protection of Farmers
For the Protection of Butchers

St. Angadrisma of Beauvais
For Rain and Protection against Drought

St. Anne
For the Protection of Horsemen, Horsewomen, and Equestrians
For the Protection of Stable Hands and Grooms

St. Ansovinus of Camerino
For the Protection of the Harvest

St. Anthony of Padua
For the General Protection of Animals and Lost Animals
For the Protection of Donkeys
For the Protection of Swine and Pigs
For the Protection of the Harvest

St. Anthony the Abbot
For the Protection of Domestic Animals
For the Protection of Swine and Pigs
For the Protection of Butchers
For the Protection of Swineherds

St. Arnulf of Soissons
For the Protection of Hop Pickers

St. Barbara
For the Protection against Storms and Lightning

St. Barnabas the Apostle
For the Protection against Hailstorms

St. Bartholomew the Apostle
For the Protection of Butchers

St. Bellinus of Padua
For Protection against Rabies

St. Benedict of Nursia
For the Protection of Bees
For the Protection of Farmers

St. Benignus of Armagh
For Protection against Worms and Parasites

St. Bernadette of Lourdes
For the Protection of Shepherds and Shepherdesses

St. Bernard of Clairvaux
For the Protection of Bees
For the Protection of Beekeepers

St. Bernard of Vienne
For the Protection of Farmers

St. Bertulph the Abbot
For Protection against Storms and Lightning

St. Beuno Gasulsych
For Protection against Diseased Cattle

St. Bieuzy of Brittany
For Protection against Rabies

St. Blaise
For Protection against Wild Animal Attacks
For the Protection of Pack Horses
For the Protection of Swine and Pigs
For the Protection of Veterinarians
For the Protection of Wool Combers

St. Botulph
For the Protection of Farmers

St. Bridget of Kildare
For the Protection of Cattle
For the Protection of Chickens and Poultry
For the Protection of Dairy Workers

St. Caesarius of Arles
For Protection against Fire

St. Castulus of Rome
For Protection against Earthquakes
For Protection against Horse Theft

St. Cataldus of Taranto
For Rain and Protection against Drought
For Protection against Storms and Lightning

St. Catherine de' Ricci
For the Protection of Tobacconists

St. Catherine of Alexandria
For the Protection of Spinners
For the Protection of Mechanics and Wheeled Vehicles

St. Catherine of Siena
For Protection against Fire

St. Charles Borromeo
For the Protection of Apple Orchards

St. Christopher
For the Protection of Gardeners
For the Protection of Fruit Dealers
For Protection against Flood

St. Coloman of Stockerau
For the Protection of Horses
For the Protection of Unmarried Farmer's Daughters

St. Columbanus
For Protection against Flood

St. Comasia
For Rain and Protection against Drought

St. Corbinian
For Protection against Bears

Sts. Crispinian and Crispin
For the Protection of Saddlemakers

St. Cunera
For the Protection of Cattle

St. Cuthman of Steyning
For the Protection of Shepherds and Shepherdesses

St. Denis of Paris
For Protection against Rabies

St. Dominic de Silo
For the Protection of Shepherds and Shepherdesses

St. Donatus of Munstereifel
For the Protection of Vintners
For Protection against Storms and Lightning

St. Dorothy of Caesarea
For the Protection of Gardeners

St. Drogo
For the Protection of Sheep and Lambs

St. Edmund of East Anglia
For Protection against Wolves

St. Eligius of Noyon
For Protection against Equine Diseases
For the Protection of Horses
For the Protection of Farriers and Hoof Trimmers
For the Protection of Mechanics and Wheeled Vehicles
For the Protection of Veterinarians

St. Elizabeth of Hungary
For the Protection of Gardens and Flower Gardens

St. Emygdius
For Protection against Earthquakes

St. Engelmaro
For the Protection of the Harvest

St. Erasmus/Elmo
For Protection against Storms and Lightning

St. Erhard of Regensburg
For Protection against Diseased Cattle

St. Eulalia of Barcelona
For Rain and Protection against Drought

St. Eustachius
For Protection against Fire

St. Felix of Nola
For Protection against Spiders

St. Fiacre
For the Protection of Gardeners

St. Florian of Lorch
For the Protection of the Harvest
For Protection against Fire
For Protection against Flood

The Four Crowned Martyrs
(Sts. Castorus, Claudius, Nicostratus, and Simpronium)
For the Protection of Cattle

St. Francis Borgia
For Protection against Earthquakes

St. Francis of Assisi
For the Protection of Domestic Animals
For the Protection of Birds
For Protection against Fire

St. Francis of Paola
For Protection against Fire

St. Friard
For Protection against Wasps

St. Gall
For the Protection of Birds
For the Protection of Chickens and Poultry

St. George
For the Protection of Horses
For the Protection of Sheep and Lambs

St. Gerlac of Valkenburg
For Protection against Diseased Cattle

St. Germaine Cousin
For the Protection of Shepherds and Shepherdesses

St. Gertrude of Nivelles
For Protection against Rodents
For the Protection of Barn Cats
For the Protection of Gardeners

Sts. Gervase and Protese
For the Protection of Haymakers

St. Giles
For the Protection of Horses
For the Protection of Rams

St. Goar of Aquitaine
For the Protection of Vintners

St. Godeberta of Noyon
For Rain and Protection against Drought

St. Gratus of Aosta
For Protection against Insects
For the Protection of Vineyards
For Protection against Storms and Lightning

St. Gregory of Ostia
For the Protection of the Harvest

St. Gregory Thaumaturgus
For Protection against Flood
For Protection against Earthquakes

St. Gualfardus of Augsburg
For the Protection of Saddlemakers

St. Gummarus
For the Protection of Cowherds

St. Gunthildis of Suffersheim
For the Protection of Cattle

St. Guy of Anderlecht
For the Protection of Horned Livestock
For the Protection of Horses
For the Protection of Stables

St. Helen
For Protection against Fire

St. Heribert of Cologne
For Rain and Protection against Drought

St. Hermengild
For Protection against Flood

St. Hervé
For Protection against Wolves

St. Hilary of Poitiers
For Protection against Snakes and Snake Bites

St. Hippolytus of Rome
For the Protection of Horses

St. Honoratus of Arles
For Rain and Protection against Drought

St. Honorius of Amiens
For the Protection of Seed, Flour, and Spice Merchants

St. Hubert of Liège
For Protection against Rabies
For the Protection of Farm Dogs

St. Isidore the Farmer
For the Protection of Livestock
For the Protection of Birds
For the Protection of Farmers
For the Protection of Rural Communities
For Rain and Protection against Drought

St. James the Greater
For the Protection of Horsemen, Horsewomen, and Equestrians
For the Protection of Veterinarians
For the Protection of Laborers

St. John Bosco
For the Protection of Laborers

St. John Chrysostom
For the Protection of Bees

St. John the Apostle
For the Protection of Butchers
For the Protection of Vintners
For the Protection of the Harvest
For Protection against Hailstorms

St. John the Baptist
For the Protection of Sheep and Lambs
For the Protection of Bird Breeders and Dealers
For Protection against Hailstorms

St. Joseph
For the Protection of Laborers
For the Protection of Domestic Homes and Farmhouses

Bl. Julian of Norwich
For the Protection of Barn Cats

St. Kevin of Glendalough
For the Protection of Cattle
For the Protection of Blackbirds
For the Protection of Geese
For the Protection of Apple Orchards

St. Lawrence
For the Protection of Butchers
For the Protection of Vintners
For Protection against Fire

St. Leonard of Noblac
For the Protection of Horses
For the Protection of Farmers

St. Louis IX
For the Protection of Distillers

St. Lucy of Syracuse
For the Protection of Farmers, Farmworkers, and Fieldhands
For Protection against Fire

St. Luke the Evangelist
For the Protection of Butchers

St. Magnus of Füssen
For Protection against Caterpillars
For Protection against Storms and Lightning

St. Marcellinus of Ancona
For Protection against Fire

St. Marcellus I
For the Protection of Stablehands and Grooms

St. Margaret of Hungary
For Protection against Flood

St. Martin de Porres
For Protection against Rodents

St. Martin of Tours
For the Protection of Horses
For the Protection of Geese
For the Protection of Vintners

St. Mary, the Blessed Virgin Mary
For the Protection of the Harvest
For the Protection of Gardens and Flower Gardens

St. Mary—the Nativity of the Blessed Virgin
For the Protection of Distillers

St. Matthew the Apostle
For the Protection of Farmers Suffering Financial Hardship

St. Maurus
For Protection against Cold Weather

St. Mawes
For Protection against Worms and Parasites

St. Medard of Noyon
For the Protection of the Harvest

St. Melangell
For the Protection of Hares and Other Small Creatures

St. Michael the Archangel
For the Protection of Grocers and Farmstands

St. Milburga
For the Protection of Birds

St. Modan
For Rain and Protection against Drought

St. Modomnoc
For the Protection of Bees

St. Morand of Cluny
For the Protection of Vintners

St. Narcissus of Girona
For Protection against Mosquitos and Biting Flies

St. Nicholas of Myra
For the Protection of Farmers
For the Protection of Butchers
For the Protection of Grain Merchants
For the Protection of Spice Merchants
For the Protection of Vintners
For the Protection of Spinners
For the Protection of Grocers and Farmstands
For Protection against Fire

St. Nicholas of Tolentino
For the Protection of Domestic Animals

St. Notburga of Eben
For the Protection of Farmers

St. Odo of Cluny
For Rain and Protection against Drought

St. Otto of Bamberg
For Protection against Rabies

Our Lady of Madhu
For Protection against Snakes and Snake Bites

Bl. Panacea of Quarona
For the Protection of Shepherds and Shepherdesses

St. Paschal Baylon
For the Protection of Shepherds and Shepherdesses

St. Patrick
For Protection against Snakes and Snake Bites
For the Protection of Organic Gardens and Farms

St. Paul the Apostle
For Protection against Snakes and Snake Bites
For the Protection of Saddlemakers
For Protection against Hailstorms

St. Perpetua
For the Protection of Cattle

St. Peter Chrysologus
For Protection against Rabies

St. Peter the Apostle
For the Protection of Butchers
For the Protection of Harvesters

St. Petka
For the Protection of Spinners

St. Pharaildis of Ghent
For the Protection of Chickens and Poultry

St. Philip Neri
For the Protection of Barn Cats

St. Phocas the Gardener
For Protection against Snakes and Snake Bites
For the Protection of Farmers
For the Protection of Gardeners

St. Ponziano of Spoleto
For Protection against Earthquakes

St. Procopius
For the Protection of Farmers

St. Raphael the Archangel
For the Protection of Shepherds and Shepherdesses

St. Regina
For the Protection of Shepherds and Shepherdesses

St. Roch
For the Protection of Farm Dogs

St. Romedio of Nonsburg
For Protection against Hailstorms

St. Rose of Lima
For the Protection of Gardeners

St. Saturninus of Toulouse
For Protection against Mad Cow Disease

St. Scholastica
For Protection against Storms and Lightning

St. Sebaldus
For Protection against Cold Weather

St. Seraphina
For the Protection of Spinners

St. Serenus the Gardener
For the Protection of Gardeners

St. Servatus of Tongres
For Protection against Rodents

St. Severinus of Noricum
For the Protection of Vineyards

St. Simeon Stylites
For the Protection of Shepherds and Shepherdesses

St. Sithney
For Protection against Rabies

St. Solange
For the Protection of Shepherds and Shepherdesses
For Rain and Protection against Drought

St. Sophia of Rome
For Protection against Frost

St. Stephen
For the Protection of Horses

St. Swithun
For Rain and Protection against Drought

Pope St. Sylvester I
For the Protection of Domestic Animals

St. Teilo of Llandaff
For the Protection of Horses

St. Thérèse of Lisieux
For the Protection of Flower Growers

St. Thomas Aquinas
For Protection against Storms and Lightning

St. Tibertius of Rome/St. Valerian
For Protection against Storms and Lightning

St. Trophimus of Arles
For Rain and Protection against Drought

St. Tryphon of Lampsacus
For Protection against Insects
For the Protection of Birds
For the Protection of Gardeners

St. Tychon of Amathus
For the Protection of Vintners

St. Uguzo of Carvagna
For the Protection of Cheese Makers

St. Ulric of Augsburg
For Protection against Rodents

St. Urban of Langres
For the Protection of Vine Dressers
For the Protection of Vintners
For Protection against Frost

St. Valentine of Rome
For the Protection of Bees
For the Protection of Beekeepers

St. Victor of Marseilles
For Protection against Storms and Lightning

St. Vincent de Paul
For the Protection of Horses

St. Vincent of Saragossa
For the Protection of Vintners

St. Vitus
For Protection against Wild Animal Attacks
For Protection against Snakes and Snake Bites
For the Protection of Early Risers and Oversleepers

St. Walburga
For the Protection of Farmers
For Protection against Storms and Lightning

St. Walstan of Bawburgh
For the Protection of Farmers

St. Walter of Pontoise
For the Protection of Stressed-Out Workers

St. Werenfridus
For the Protection of Gardeners

Permissions

Every reasonable effort has been made to determine copyright holders of excerpted materials and to secure permissions as needed. If any copyright materials have been inadvertently used in this work without proper credit being given in one form or another, please notify Loyola Press in writing so that future printings of this work may be corrected accordingly.

About the Author

Andie Andrews Eisenberg is a recreational horseback rider, certified equine massage therapist, screenwriter, cowgirl poet, novelist, blogger, sheep farmer, and novice homesteader. Several years ago, she moved from suburbia to a small hobby farm in New Jersey so that Hook, her beloved Quarter Horse gelding and muse for one of her novels, could come home to live with her happily ever after. She has since moved a little farther afield to Middle Tennessee, where she homesteads with her tractor-happy husband, Ed, and twenty hens, two sassy mares, a small flock of sheep (www.allsaintsvalaisblacknosesheep.com), and a gregarious Golden Retriever/farm-dog-in-training. When she's not writing, Andie can be found kicking up dust while dancing with horses, tending gardens, chasing chickens, cuddling lambs, mending fences, sweeping the barn, feeding her family, and finding 101 uses for baling twine around the farm.